D1482256

AMERICAN FAMILY POLICY

content and context

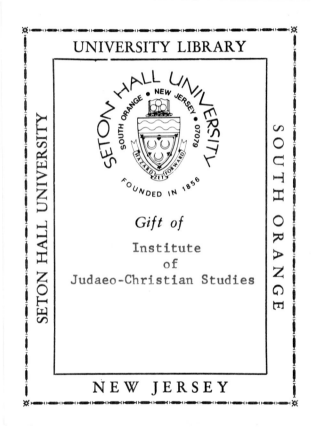

AMERICAN
FAMILY
POLICY

content

and

context

ROBERT M. RICE

Family Service Association of America
New York

HQ
536
R47

Library of Congress Cataloging in Publication Data

Rice, Robert M.   1930-
  American family policy.

  Bibliography: p. 136
  Includes index.
    1. Family—United States.   2. United States—
Social policy.   I. Title.
HQ536.R47   301.42'0973   77-15664
ISBN   0-87304-160-7

Printed in the United States of America

Designed by Patricia Ryan

 3

To Dr. Douglas Bunker, of the State University of New York at Buffalo, Center for Policy Studies, whose encouragement and intelligent criticism sustained this work.

And to Priscilla, Thad, Dorie, and Robin, who regularly remind me of how important families really are.

PREFACE

The Family Service Association of America is pleased to publish this book by Robert M. Rice on *American Family Policy: Content and Context*. Rice is a valued colleague. He has been a practitioner, an administrator, a consultant, and is now a policy formulator in the family field. From the time we first began to know one another well, in 1967, Rice and I have been discussing the impact of the American political and corporate systems on family life and the need for a comprehensive, coherent, and explicit family policy in the United States as a basis for developing programs, services, and activities concerned with the family.

Like Rice, I grew up as a practitioner of family casework in family service agencies. I continue to hold a strong belief in the efficacy of individualized services to families in general and family casework in particular. Early on, however, I was struck by the need for families to adapt constantly to social, political, corporate, and other systems, and the heavy demands made by these systems on families. I wondered why it was that these systems rarely asked themselves, "How do we affect families and how might we behave in the best interest of strong family life?" It was this kind of questioning which led me originally to become a "case advocate" for the families with whom I worked. By this, I mean trying to bend the systems to work for my families. Later, with the help of some very astute colleagues, I began to see the significance of systems change, so that the systems which had an impact on families might work for all families. This kind of thinking ultimately invaded the whole of the family service movement and gave birth to the practice of family advocacy. The link between family casework and family advocacy, although apparent to some initially, was missed by others. Rather than being seen as a continuum of services for, with, and on behalf of families, some saw a dichotomy which, in my opinion, never existed, except in the lack of understanding of the systems approach to the family.

Fortunately, today there is less consideration of a dichotomy between casework and family advocacy and more of the essential nature of both working together. We are now looking even further and the complementary role of family policy development is gaining recognition as a significant tool for strengthening family life. In the family service movement, we are beginning to see a joining of individualized services, advocacy, and policy in the interests of all families. We are indebted for this important evolutionary development, not only to serious students of the family and to policy scientists such as Rice, who have a deep and abiding interest and concern about American families, but also to certain of our political and corporate leaders who share this concern. It is, therefore, in the interest of the ultimate development of a comprehensive, coherent, and explicit family policy that FSAA chose to publish this book.

It is the hope of FSAA that *American Family Policy: Content and Context* will be widely read by practitioners, advocates, administrators, volunteer leaders, corporate policymakers, and government policy developers and framers. Further, it is hoped that, in the reading, a clearer understanding will be gained of what family policy is and why its development is important to the future of the American family, to our humanity, and to our democratic society.

W. KEITH DAUGHERTY
General Director
Family Service Association of America
New York, N.Y.

FOREWORD

In recent years, there has been a dramatic and widespread increase in interest in American families generally, and in the ways in which they are affected by public policy specifically. A broad range of organizations and individuals have been actively discussing, studying, and exploring this subject, often with quite different perspectives and understandings.

The academic and research communities have devoted a markedly growing proportion of their attention and energies to this issue. The media contain a new emphasis on family-related news and developments. And there is unprecedented and bipartisan interest by political and governmental leaders in finding ways to make public policies more supportive of families. Indeed, both major political parties made this task one of their explicit priorities in last fall's Presidential election. The present administration and Congress have already agreed to and enacted a major public service jobs program designed in part to strengthen families. The objective of supporting families is one of the fundamental goals of the pending legislation proposals to reform both the welfare and foster care systems, and President Carter will convene the first-ever White House Conference on Families in 1979.

In *American Family Policy: Content and Context*, Bob Rice has provided us with a thorough but succinct discussion of the parameters and substance of the subject. His review of family function theory, current trends in family life, and the history of and influences on family policy add needed depth and perspective to the current activities in this area.

He begins with a discussion of what the family is and how it functions, which includes a review of the work of several theorists and the development of his own typology of these functions and how they are changing. This background information provides a particularly valuable introduction to those of us who are not academic experts in this field.

His next chapter summarizes a range of research studies and statistics on the status of the modern American family, adding a depth of analysis about current trends that are frequently overlooked by those who focus on more spectacular data, for example, those related solely to divorce rates. This chapter contains a particularly thought-provoking section about the lack of available knowledge on the family as a consuming unit.

Chapters three and four focus on what the author calls the "family policymaking environment" and "family policy proposals" respectively, and brings together a wealth of information about both the activities and the actors in policymaking arenas relevant to families. It is here that he documents and explains the fact that "comprehensive policy toward the family does not now exist in either federal or state government in the United States" and that "in the United States . . . the family is avoided as an explicit object of public policymaking." He describes the role of various professions and human services in terms of their influences on and support of (or lack of support of) family-oriented approaches to services provision, and discusses the role of contemporary social movements—summarizing these to illustrate the lack of cohesion around family issues. His effort to delineate the roles and approaches of private service and advocacy groups, which are too often omitted in policy treatises, is especially helpful. And he adds an extremely important historical perspective with his explanation of the philosophical premises in American democracy which have excluded a family perspective in past policymaking.

The author is optimistic, however, about the future development of national family policy due to increased national interest in the topic and the development of constituencies for the family. In his final chapter, he outlines his recommendations for the components of a national family policy. While I do not agree with all of his proposals—including specifically any implication that we should seek to develop "a single, national, comprehensive family policy," and the suggestion that a "family bureau within government" should be created—I find this book to be of tremendous value in articulating, discussing, and explaining a variety of forces, trends, and attitudes that affect policies relevant to families. Above all, I support and applaud his emphasis on the need to understand and respect the pluralism and diversity of families in this country; his appreciation of the resilience of families; his recognition that families are changing, not breaking down; and his statement that the appropriate role of society and government with respect to families is to help discover how to "protect and enrich families, not harass and disorient them." And, of couse, I agree completely with his conclusion that "we need to develop information on how government already has an impact on the family."

In summary, this timely book brings together in one place a wide range of facts and perspectives on families and policies affecting families, a thoughtful analysis of many of the reasons America has not adopted an explicit family policy, and a series of specific recommendations about what a national family policy might include. It can make a significant contribution to the debate and dialogue about, and any ultimate progress toward, the development of public policies which realistically, explicitly, and sensitively address the needs of American families. I commend it to the attention of anyone interested in gaining a deeper and more complete understanding of many of the issues involved in the current and growing interest in families and family-related policies.

A. SIDNEY JOHNSON, III
Director, Family Impact Seminar,
George Washington University,
Washington, D.C.

CONTENTS

INTRODUCTION

The phrase "national family policy" is increasingly used in discussions about domestic policy in the United States to convey the idea of a single policy direction which is comprehensive, coherent, and explicit and which guides governmental activities concerned with the family. The concept of such macropolicy is of fairly recent origin and has gone through certain developmental stages. The bulk of the writing on the subject has tended to express rather narrow program concepts that observers have deemed crucial for helping the family. Very recently, a few more general statements, conceptualized more comprehensively, have begun to appear.

There are reasons for the increased interest in this subject. Domestic legislation in the 1960s was oriented particularly toward program development. Various programs were established without due consideration to their interrelationships, and many of them came to be in conflict with other programs and goals. Disappointment with this categorical approach caused policymakers to be more sensitive to the context of program proposals. There is a natural link between comprehensive policy formation and turning away from the categorical approach.

The 1970s have also been characterized by considerable public concern with ethics and values as expressed in the public arena. A "post-Watergate morality" has led Americans to examine ethical standards in American life generally. One object of concern has been an alleged breakdown of American family life, and demographic data have shown rapidly increasing divorce rates, an increase in the proportion of single-parent families, and a declining marriage rate. It has been easy to use these data to demonstrate moral decline, and, in response, a politic has been developed expressing concern about the family.

The time now seems to have arrived for a reexamination both of the role of the family in American society and of the relationship between government and the family. This book is intended to contribute to a clarification of the emerging stream of thought in these areas in relation to comprehensive family policy in the United States.

Policymaking is ultimately an intensely political process involving many actors in a process of negotiation; it is, therefore, not entirely a rational process. The matter of establishing some guidelines for the process of policy determination ("metapolicy," as it is termed in this book), is particularly relevant as the family becomes increasingly important in public affairs. Although much has been written about the need for developing a comprehensive family policy on the national level, there have been few attempts to define what that policy might contain.

The material presented here provides a rationale for the family to become a target for public policymaking. The family is regarded as a crucial social institution that functions both as a dependent and an independent variable in a continuing exchange process with the larger society. There is evidence here that socially determined changes are deeply disturbing to familial patterns. Metapolicy leading toward mobilization for policymaking is defined. It is hoped that this book will contribute to setting in motion a policymaking process directed to the American family, a matter which is becoming essential to the preservation of a society that can remain responsive to both individual and collective human needs.

chapter 1

FAMILY FUNCTIONS AS LINKS WITH MODERN AMERICAN SOCIETY

American Family Policy: The ideal of family is sacrosanct for most Americans, who of course want their government to support family life. But do they? American family policy is in fact underdeveloped, and there are indications that the very idea can bring out deeply conflicting notions of what is—and is not—good and proper for family life.

"Family" conjures up visions of God, motherhood, and apple pie. Yet God has been proclaimed deceased, motherhood has been attacked as a form of slavery, and apple pie contains cholesterol and calories dangerous for human consumption. The family has been disdained as outmoded by some.

Even more important, Americans have reserved their family lives as last preserves of privacy. To consider public policy toward the family might enlarge the domain of government beyond the limit of a freedom-loving people's endurance. "The family is one place where the government should have a hands-off policy" is a repeated cocktail-party comment. Few, it seems, would wish their personal lives to be further regulated by an intrusive government.

To discuss the need for a policy response to the family requires reaching back to the nature of the family, its ties to a wider society, and indicators of how well it performs its functions. It is necessary to understand how the family acts as a component of society and to learn enough about divergence of family forms to develop a sense of what is, and what is not, private and distinct from society at large about the family. There is a need to understand what may be compelling about the notion of policy as applied to the family, and, finally, to look at what such policy might contain and avoid.

Public policy is essentially an effort to adjust society's management of its components. The family is a major component of nearly all societies, one of the most basic of all social institutions. A recent report of the International Union of Family Organizations states that the family is a universal reality, that it is "recognized everywhere as being the basic unit or fundamental cell of society," despite its pluralism of forms.[1] Moreover, the family functions in many ways—on a biological level, in terms of emotions and interpersonal relations, in education and socialization, and in economics. The family is defined as intermediate between the "microcosm and the macrocosm" (the individual and the larger society); it is affected by the rapid change taking place both in highly industrialized and urbanized societies and in developing countries. The report concludes that the strength of the family is related to social progress.

VIEWS OF THE FAMILY

There is an old argument over the universality of the family as an institution. George Peter Murdock is a great defender of the universality of the family form.[2] His view, however, has been challenged by efforts to find a society without a family form, often leading to esoteric arguments concerning the definitions of family.[3] Robert F. Winch, refuting the Murdock argument, states ". . . it does not seem necessary to conclude that the existence of a familial system . . . is necessary for the existence of a society."[4] The enormous variety of family life experience, as expressed among both individual families and societies, leads to equivocation among investigators, leaving unanswered questions about the relationship of the family to society despite continued agreement that the family is in some way deeply related to societal formation.

If the family is an important unit of society, to what degree is it a product of society and to what degree does it produce social effects? Virginia McLaughlin questions the apparent truism that an industrial society can decimate a family institution geared to rural life.[5] Her studies suggest that the family functions as an independent variable capable of affecting the economy. Conversely, John McKnight has described the family as a scapegoat for society's ills, in view of the common tendency to blame the family for causing that which actually affects it![6]

This apparent confusion seems best answered by those who describe a process of interchange between the family and the societal environment. Norman W. Bell and Ezra F. Vogel provide a model for functional analysis of interchange between the nuclear family and the economy, the polity, the community, and the societal value system.[7] Bell and Vogel have undertaken a major overview of a broad range of writings and they differentiate three functions of the family.[8] The first examines the exchange between the nuclear family and other social systems. The second deals with internal exchange as forming part of family activities. And the third concerns the relationship between family and personality development. In these categories, the following subfunctions are identified: task performance, family leadership, integration and solidarity, and the family value system.

Task performance includes processes concerning and surrounding consumption, caretaking roles with those family members who are dependent, establishing affective relationships and developing a guidance system for them, distributing labor, adapting to what is available for living requirements, and providing recognition for tasks performed. There is a rich social and emotional climate contained in these transactions which produces enormous variety both in the tasks carried out and in the effect of those tasks upon individual members and society.

Complex patterns of the development of *family leadership* may or may not be related to task performance. Leadership patterns may include the entire family, a member or members of the family assigned the decision-making process, or, for that matter, the turning over of decisions to established outsiders. Changing power relationships continue throughout the life of the family as personal changes in maturation take place. Rules, often unconscious, for decision making become established.

Some degree of *integration and solidarity* is necessary within the family unit to maintain close relationships between members over a long period of time. Manifestations of solidarity may include ritual and celebration or common symbols. Possessions often take on symbolic value as do common memories and established patterns of behavior. Sanctions may punish deviance. Some of these, such as taboos, can be very strong, while others, such as family customs, are less powerful. The establishment of family solidarity and the accompanying deep personal bonds have a major effect upon personality formation of family members.

Families establish their own *value systems*, which are somehow related to a larger social value orientation. Although there is usually considerable room for adjustment available to individual family members, frequently there are shared normative beliefs throughout the family. Shadings of what is considered legitimate and illegitimate behavior may become quite subtle and may differ from consciously stated norms. Values may be used for slowing the process of change and maintaining patterns of behavior, but, because the family is a small group with informal ties, the family value system may be quite flexible, perhaps considerably more so than the society that surrounds it.

FAMILY CHANGE

Bell and Vogel present a broad description of family functions across societal and cultural lines, but they do not account for another aspect of family function—change. Much of the literature concerning family function accentuates the change process in the American family. Often, such discussion includes an analysis which demonstrates the family's response to industrialism. William F. Ogburn, for example, saw that much of the functional productivity of the family had given way to corporate industry.[9] In fact, the family had lost many functions. Formal education had become a function of the school and not of the informal family group. The family's protective functions had been turned over to such civic forces as the police. Authority was no longer lodged in parents but rather in employers, government officials, and other representatives of formally organized groupings. Religious instruction had been turned over to the church or had been given short shrift in comparison to the part it had played earlier as a central function of the family. Organized recreation was replacing family orientation to play. A major function of the family in past times—the process of passing status from person to person and generation to generation—had little importance as status became more a product of work experience, income, and education.

Although Ogburn emphasized the losses in family functions, he did see a concomitant rise in "personality functions," which he described as the mutual adjustment of family members and their adaptation to the outside world through family experience. Thus, he saw the family as becoming more concerned with the individuals within it; in his phraseology, the family was moving from being an institution to being a less formalized grouping structured to meet the needs of individual members. This theme is constantly echoed today. The family geared to the individual is not only described but even celebrated.[10]

THEORIES ON FAMILY LIFE CYCLE AND FUNCTIONAL DECLINE

The tasks that a family performs at various stages of its existence are very important in any analysis of family functions. Sometimes called family life cycle theory, sometimes stage theory, the literature dealing with task analysis derives largely from areas concerning therapy or treatment of the family rather than study of the family as a social institution. It is utilized as a means to establish norms by which family therapists measure degrees of family dysfunction. Marc Sheinbein has recently reviewed this theory, in which the emphasis is on task performance. He states:

In this context, the normal crises in family life development can be itemized with the expected chronological age range in which each might occur. The development task of each generation seems to pass through the following crises, or series of separations: birth, leaving mother (around ages one to six), leaving home (around ages four to twelve), leaving the family (around ages ten to twenty), beginning one's own family (around ages eighteen to twenty-five), producing one's own children (usually after age twenty), and losing one's own children through repetition of the series. Other significant separations are losses through death, divorce, and abandonment. . . . The major thesis is that each crisis has an enormously complex set of antecedents and consequents both for the family system and for the interrelated members.[11]

Other views help to define and to tighten concepts of family function. One view concerns the common notion of declining family function in an industrial society. Conversely, J. Richard Udry has insisted that increased function is derived from the smaller number of functions the family now performs.[12] If there are fewer functions, he contends, they may exert a greater effect upon the individual family member.

PROBLEMS IN FUNCTIONAL ANALYSIS

Bell and Vogel pose a series of problems for functional analysis in regard to definitions.[13] They indicate that functions differ with reference to the relationship between the family and the social system. That is, the family may differ in function in regard to an individual member from what it may do with reference to society as a whole or to a subsystem of society. There is also the nagging definitional question about the family under consideration and whether it is nuclear or extended.

Certainly, problems in establishing definitive labels do exist. The effort here, however, is not to join in definitional arguments but to develop some fairly broad statements about family function that will advance family policy development.

Some further problems exist in identifying family function, and a major one involves the changeability of the structure of the family. Few individuals remain forever in a single type of family structure, although most have had some experiences in the traditional nuclear family.[14] Not only is there pluralism of family form and pluralism in the forms the individual member experiences, but also there is structural change in the continuity of the single family as the separation of members, whether voluntary or involuntary, occurs. The nature of family function, or the balance of several functions, may change along with the change in structure. Over time, discontinuity is an aspect of most family experience.

The mechanics of family function relate to the choices families make. The opportunities for making choices vary greatly in our society and in many ways are a function of socioeconomic class. Martin B. Sussman describes the problem of "option glut" as an extreme comparison of the way in which higher class families may become dysfunctional, just as lower class families may become incapacitated by a poverty of choice.[15]

TYPOLOGIES OF FAMILY FUNCTION

Despite the many difficulties, typologies of family function are not at all uncommon. Furthermore, there are marked similarities among them.

For purposes of discussion and as a means of summarizing rather diverse writing on the subject of family function, a functional typology is utilized here. The family is viewed as an outlet for *expression and affection,* as a means for *socialization and enculturation,* as a source of *continuity,* as a special means for *interaction with environment,* and as a center of *consumption.*

EXPRESSION AND AFFECTION

Much of the content of functional change in modern family life can be understood by considering the strong trend toward emphasis on affective and expressive modes within the family. A central fact of industrialization is the movement of the centers of production from small primary groups, often families or family-related groups, to larger bureaucratic groups. Thus, in earlier times the family was closely connected with productive or instrumental tasks, but these tasks have been removed in today's industrialized societies. In the process, emotional bonds have come to replace work relationships related to physical survival.

The family has come to emphasize internal emotional exchanges with high expectations for self-satisfaction. Helen Frank has written about the "self-actualization ethic" that has come to permeate idealism concerning the family.[16] Problems result when a happiness ethic does not include a sense of social responsibility, and Frank is not alone in sounding an alarm about the degree of emphasis on hedonistic principles and their shortcomings as central directions for family function and meaning for family members. Richard E. Farson sees the change more positively and indicates that the emphasis upon affect within the family fills an important gap in society, so that the family will "become a rehabilitative agent, a buffer against a very complex and demanding world in which family members constitute our only advocates, the only people who are for us. So we shall depend upon them increasingly."[17]

However one values the matter, the emotionality of the family seems to compensate for the pressure to rationalize relationships in the industrial society. Bureaucratic organization, a central characteristic of industrialization, has stressed productive, rational relationships among people. This stance has meant that the family has become the institution which, for many, is the center of affective human experience.

If, however, industrialization produces and ultimately supports the emotion-focused family, it also sets limits on the extent to which the family can meet its emotional needs. This can produce sanctions which can seriously disturb emotional homeostatsis,[18] and often these limits and impingments are experienced as family failure.

SOCIALIZATION AND ENCULTURATION

Although they are not identical processes, socialization and enculturation are treated together here. Socialization as a family function is that process by which the young learn to pattern their behavior on cultural norms. (There is growing interest in adult phases of socialization, but this is not discussed here.) Enculturation is a somewhat broader term, involving the process by which a fit is established between an individual and his society, not only because of what he learns or how he behaves, but also because of the social roles assigned to him.

The family does not have an exclusive role to play in either socialization or enculturation. In fact, these family functions have become increasingly shared with other institutions. It is often through looking at these functions that observers perceive functional loss for the family in industrialized society. Winch has described family function regarding maturation as follows:

The child moves from dependency on the family to meet its physical needs in the direction of relying on the family to meet its psychic needs. As part of early nurturing the child needs emotional warmth provided unconditionally. Gradually, the child's behavior must be controlled, restrained, and directed in order to begin the process of becoming socially acceptable. The child must then move toward the process of task and skill development of increasing complexity. Most children are cared for within a family structure from immediately following birth. The unconstrained nurturing process therefore is the product of the family and has not yet given way to institutional auspices. A considerable body of research suggests that this early experience between the infant and the family is extremely important; it cannot be adequately substituted through institutional means.[19]

Nevertheless, there has been strong pressure in the United States for massive day care programs available to children at very early ages, although this movement has remained politically controversial and theoretically questionable.[20] The point is that there is an organized effort to intrude upon the family's excusivity in providing child care at the youngest ages.

There has been a great deal of both competition and sharing between the family and other organized groupings in later stages of the child's socialization. Schools have had much to do with building socially useful behavioral controls and have had a primary role in teaching skills. In fact, the school experience is usually the institutional basis for the child's emancipation from his family.

It has sometimes been argued that the preindustrial family had exclusive control of the function of socialization and that, in this regard, there is an absolute change between preindustrial and postindustrial society. It is clear, however, that the school has become a major force in socialization of the young in areas once the prerogative of the family; and children can experience discontinuities as they move between the two environments.[21]

Although the family is supported for its socialization function, its function of ascribing status tends to be at odds with the Horatio Alger myth. Considerable data suggest that status ascription, even in the supposedly open society in the United States, remains correlated with inherited family status. One of the few un-contested conclusions of the controversial Moynihan Report is the evidence for the family's status-conferring function.[22] There is considerable evidence that it is a pervasive factor in American class structure,[23] and much of the controversy surrounding the question of the family's utility in modern society derives from this fact. Winch has suggested that social class mobility becomes most available following emancipation from one's family of origin, and it is the adult phase of living that opens society beyond the assignment of status first established by family membership.[24] Nonetheless, the family acts as a conservative force in maintaining patterns of class assumption and behavior.

The assignment of legitimacy is another family function, and one that has assumed an importance far beyond the apparent one of dealing with the problem of bastardy. The family legitimates a care relationship between its members that is of extreme importance to society and provides a psychological point of origin for its individual members. As a result of this function of legitimizing, a body of family law has developed.

Like so many aspects of family function, status ascription within the family is not a process directed to identical goals by various families, or even identical goals within the same family. Bernard Farber suggests two different kinship patterns with opposing functions.[25] In the *centripetal* form, the family attempts to stratify the community while endeavoring to develop its own power and wealth. Thus, the family becomes a power base to manipulate other institutions. Contrastingly, in the *centrifugal* form, the family is used to diffuse power and wealth throughout a territory. According to this form, family norms are subordinated when they conflict with those of other institutions and the family loses its capacity as a power base. Behavior patterns support these social functions. It is Farber's view that both centripetal and centrifugal forms exist in all societies, but that they have different prevalences.

Allan Schnaiberg and Sheldon Goldenberg caution that ascription of status is not a one-way process, that children make an impact upon the parents' status, and that this is particularly true in lower socioeconomic class behavior.[26] In this sense, the family may become a vehicle for class mobility. These writers even question some of the assumptions common in our society that smaller families will aid in the social mobility of the poor, indicating that often poor parents are materially aided in life by successful offspring.

It would appear that the functions of socialization and enculturation place the family in the position of being a building block of society. As such, the family may be a force for change or pattern maintenance, rigidity or mobility. Its functional activities are multifaceted, as is the society within which it functions. For example, the family increasing shares the socialization process with formal organizations, notably schools. Families function neither monolithically nor unilaterally, but rather interact with other variables. The interaction of multiple societal forces holds the potential for effectiveness and also for conflict.

CONTINUITY

No other institution spans the years of life as does the family. In this sense, the functioning family, although it may change in form, is a source of continuity. During an individual's lifetime, the family both meets his dependency needs and expects him to provide care to other family members. Thus, continuity has to do with the psychological issue of a sense of roots and purpose, the social issue of care for dependency, and the structural issue of kinship.

The matter of continutiy must be examined in relation to the extended family, because it is through this extension of the nuclear family that intergenerational family ties are built and the "family" remains, while the nuclear family undergoes change. It is through kinship links that children retain ties with their parents after their own emancipation. It is also the means by which the old can maintain a sense of family after their own generation dies. Until fairly recently, it was believed that the extended family was a casualty of modern society. William J. Goode, for example, describes the extended family as a product of rural society, functional primarily because it had not yet been supplanted by more formal organizations.[27] It is not surprising, therefore, that he feels that the old have become umimportant in American life.[28] Talcott Parsons and Renee C. Fox found the extended family losing its care functions to health care institutions.[29]

Lately, however, there has been some renewed interest in the extended family and its care-giving possibilities; and there is reason for both optimism and pessimism about the importance and continuance of the extended family. The intervening variables of ethnicity and religion, rural and urban differences, and social class factors cloud the picture. What is important, however, is that there continues to be an extended family function that operates throughout a considerable part of the culture and that maintains a sense of continuity for many.

INTERACTION WITH THE ENVIRONMENT

Goode has described the family and industrial factors as independent but interacting variables.[30] In his view, industrial forces do not entirely shape the family, as the family has a tendency to resist them; however, family processes do gradually change to meet the needs of an industrial environment. By the same token, industry slowly and resistively reacts to family forces, gradually accommodating enough of them to ensure that family members may take part in the industrial system.[31]

Sussman carries the point further. He describes the family in terms of mediation with the environment.[32] In fact, he believes the skill of the family in performing the mediation function to be correlated with the social success of its members. He considers this function to be most important when the family exists within a bureaucratic socity. Mediation, a function of both the nuclear and the extended kin networks, "has to involve action which results in compromise without an undue loss of position, integrity, or power by participants. It involves a reciprocal process of being able to influence as well as being influenced."[33] The family member whose family performs the mediation function poorly must turn to bureaucratic officials, and these officials must carry out bureaucratic goals and favor them over those of the individual. In this sense, the family can be more fully on the side of one of its members than can any organized structure that derives from a bureaucracy.

In some kin networks, certain family members act in semi- official capacities, gaining status by their capacity to mediate with bureaucracies. This is particularly true among deprived ethnic minorities, in which individuals become advocates for other family members.[34]

Bell and Vogel tend to view this function in terms of a general exchange between the environment and the family.[35] They describe a series of tradeoffs between the family and the institutions that surround it. For example, the family may conform to societal norms; in return the larger society offers the reward of approval and legitimacy. Such exchanges are repeated and modified, with each party being affected by the specifics of each exchange. The family is thus seen as an early force in the organization of its individual members, a kind of subsociety.

This description of exchange presents a more peaceful homeostasis compared to the more conflict-laden view in which the individual family member requires the advocacy of the family in his confrontations with the outside world. In both cases, however, the family is seen as a pivot in the exchange between the individual and the institutions that affect him and thereby explain data correlations between indicators of family solidarity and the social success of family members.

CONSUMPTION

It could be argued that the family function of consumption and participation in the economy is a special form of the interchange between the family and the social institutions discussed above. It is treated separately because it is a particularly significant interaction within an industrial society.

Udry flatly states that the nuclear family is the basic consumption unit of the economy, but Peter Moock has observed that much economic theory has been unable to explain with precision the family as a consumer.[36] Traditional economic concepts have treated the consumer as an individual rather than considering the interactions of a group such as the family. More recently, however, greater attention has been paid to the family as a consuming unit, and one theory views the family "as a cohesive and consistent decision-making unit, which allocates the time of different family members in combination with purchased articles in order to produce desired commodities."[37] Here, consumption is seen as an activity used in *combination* with internal time allocations, and the definition of commodities equates them with values. This explains why the family is apt to purchase quality over quantity as its income rises. It also means that commodities are seldom purchased for themselves, but rather support values and activities such as the raising of children.

Bell and Vogel describe a process of interchange between the nuclear family and the economy, the family engaging in the production process through allocation of time by family members for work, and in turn consuming the products of the economy.[38] According to this view, the success with which the family can support the employment and work of its members becomes related to its consumption capacities, just as high consumption produces the need for work performance by family members.

Other efforts have been made to understand the consumption process within families, including an attempt to produce a typology of consumption patterns related to the relative expectations of husband and wife,[39] and efforts to understand the meaning of women's work, both paid and unpaid.[40] Perhaps the most authoritative body of knowledge about economic processes within families resides within the domain of law, which recognizes the family as a vehicle for handling property that takes precedence over most claims. Thus, family economic functions regarding, for example, inheritance and interlocked financial resources, as expressed in tax law, maintain and support as well as reflect actual family practice. Thus, economic theory detailing the place of the family in the economy has some peculiar qualities. Although it is generally understood that the family makes a major contribution to the economy, the perceptions of the mechanics involved vary considerably.

HISTORICAL VIEW OF THE EFFECTS OF INDUSTRIALIZATION

In developing the above typology of family function, the importance of industrialization has been mentioned repeatedly. It has been noted that certain instrumental functions have either disappeared or have become less exclusively the function of the family and are shared with other organized groups. The idea persists that industrialization had a major effect upon family function and that the family as it is known today is considerably different from that institution as it might have appeared in a preindustrial society. A discussion of family function, therefore, is incomplete without an examination of the contribution of the social historian.

Historical interest in the family is a relatively new pursuit connected with the current interest in folk history, as contrasted with the older historical interest in formal societies and government.[41] Social historians go to innovative and unexpected sources for data, not to the official records of nations. For example, the ways in which families have been depicted in art, information on gravestones, physicians' records, records of property transactions, diaries, and so forth, all prove to be legitimate sources for the new social historian. It would appear that the social indicators movement has had some effect upon this developing school, the approach being similar to a search for indicators of how populations actually lived. Data sources are apt to be of unproved validity, and most social historians tend to caution that their conclusions and choices of data sources do not meet scientific criteria. As a result, there has been some exceedingly intense criticism of the historical approach to the family.[42] Although these correctives to traditional theory are not without controversy, they provide a perspective that enriches perceptions of family function, particularly in relation to the effects of industrialization.

One clear challenge from this kind of research is to the notion that the family was somehow better or purer prior to industrialization. Functions of the family have shifted, but in historical terms this change is not so clearly a "breakdown" as some writers have suggested. The modern family thus can be perceived as a social adaptation to modern society, still in transition, dynamic, but with new stress points. Family function can then be viewed as a reaction to the fit between society, individuals, and the family grouping itself.

The functions of the family reveal certain similarities or continuities in the preindustrial and the postindustrial eras, but there are also discontinuities or shifts in the functions of and attitudes toward the family. What is remarkable is that the continuities and discontinuities differ radically, at least in some instances, from those described in some of the earlier sociological writings which presupposed how industrialization had affected the family. Part of the change that has taken place in understanding family function concerns the ability to take a longer historical perspective on what has happened.

Personal alienation or loneliness among family members is not solely a response to modern social conditions as some writers have indicated. The causes of alienation may have changed, but discontinuities in relationships between family members, often caused by death, were very much a part of the preindustrial family experience. Because of the prevalance of disease, as Peter Laslett points out, early death was common, "broken homes" were often the result, and remarriage was common.[43] It was also not uncommon for children from intact families to live in other people's homes during their minority.[44]

Another common element in preindustrial and postindustrial families is the emphasis upon the nuclear family.[45] Despite the fact that kin groupings and extended families had certain instrumental importance and subsequent formalization of relationships which are less common in modern times, historical data suggest that the nuclear, conjugal family was the grouping most people associated with the concept of family.

Personal mobility, sometimes regarded as a force in modern life which transformed the preindustrial family form into the modern family form, is not an exclusive quality of modern society. It appears that there was considerable mobility in family life long before full industrialization.[46] For Americans, at least, mobility has been a fact of family life for several centuries.

None of this should suggest that change has not occurred within the family as society has changed. In fact, the discontinuities in family life are quite striking. Social historian Philippe Aries has examined minute details of European medieval historical data and develops a central conclusion that childhood is a concept embraced by moderns but not shared by their medieval ancestors.[47] Because of the necessary emphasis upon the instrumental qualities of the family, Aries suggests, children did not take on particular meaning until they were able to participate in the work life of the family. Furthermore, in those times it was emotionally necessary to avoid too great an emphasis upon affective ties with children because of the high death rate for the very young. Thus, children were largely ignored and were finally accepted into the family only as young adults who could carry out necessary familial and productive tasks. Otherwise, they were often treated as playthings, and, in modern terms, often abusively. Wet nursing, boarding out, and subsequently indenture became possible because of these conditions, and institutions were formed that reinforced the possibilities of separation between parent and child.

Edward Shorter repeatedly points out that depth of affection was an impossibility in the somewhat grim physical environment of preindustrial society, that marriage was often devoid of great feeling, that eroticism tended to be limited to youth, and that family members were absorbed primarily with the issue of survival, not with affectional ties.[48] In Shorter's view, industrialization allowed the family to become the center for affection, whereas in preindustrial society emotional life was spread among many community groups, with no particular emphasis upon the family as a place to express depth of feelings. The modern emphasis on affection has allowed for a major shift in matters of marital preference. An individual contemplating marriage no longer needs to depend on arrangements made through parental negotiations, connected with kin networks. He or she can now exert personal choice in selecting a marital partner.[49] Also, in the past, marital behavior was much more dependent upon external controls, in that government could exert considerable authority over behavior within the nuclear family.[50]

Kinship relationships have become quite different from what they were in pre-modern times. Thus some writers who have assumed that kinship networks have experienced loss due to modernization have the problem of comparing dissimilar affectional relationships. Shorter indicates that while negotiations with kin were common, there was little interest in kin as people.[51] Today's family includes the kin network in its affectional relationships.

Historical writings indicate, therefore, that the prevalence of illness and death at early age, coupled with the degree of effort required merely to survive, produced a family heavily armored against the expression of deep affection but capable of carrying out productive functions. The preindustrial family had to be ready for sudden loss of relationships. Marriages usually could not last as long as their modern counterparts nor could people generally expect to reach old age. Thus, the historians illustrate that the modern family has become possible only as a result of the forces of industrialization. A functional form of the family has evolved which, in some ways, is highly ambitious compared to earlier forms. It expects to hold together over more years and expects high returns for its members in emotional well-being; it also must function as an important source of interchange between the individual family member and the society around him. It has resources available to it that preindustrial families did not have—housing which allows for privacy, medicine to deal with sickness, schooling and training to deal effectively with social institutions, and an ethos which is not intrusive. Shorter has commented, concerning the new marital opportunities:

> . . . and yet if I am right, one price paid for this new capacity to explore one's sensory responses has been the abandonment of a meaningful emotional life outside the home. Another price is a vastly increased instability in marital relations. A final price of the eroticization of the couple's life, both before marriage and after, is the disintegration of a sense of the lineage of the family. Nothing is free in this world.[52]

chapter 2

INDICATORS OF FAMILY TRENDS

As defined here, social indicators are *statistics* chosen because they are indices of the reality of family behavior. The focus of these statistics is on the measurements of family functioning after 1970. The effort was made not only to be current, but also to reflect what appears to be fairly universal macrosocietal change between the 1970s and the 1960s.

In the choice of statistics presumed to be significant for understanding what is happening to families and family behavior, certain guidelines have been used. (1) Large-scale studies utilizing either near-universal or representative-sample methods are preferred. (2) Data chosen are suggestive of how the family is functioning in society. Statistics concerning the use of welfare or other social programs are not utilized because they are apt to be measures of the program activity rather than a characterization of the behavior of families. (3) Data are chosen which reflect change. The availability of time series is extremely important, but time series derived from surveys are scarce.

The first significant effort to develop social indicators specifically about family life occurred at the beginning of the current decade, when the Russell Sage Foundation financed a study based on 1960s data.[1] This work primarily used census data, both to discuss previous family performance and as a means of establishing predictors. The work, carried out by Abbott B. Ferriss, is highly descriptive and objective, but as Ferriss admits, there are limitations to the organization of the material because it is not directed toward the function of family in society but rather emphasizes instead that which is available in census material. The continuing problem of getting qualitative rather than quantitative measurements which Ferriss identifies remains apparent in the data collection in this chapter.

BROAD SOCIETAL CHANGES

The target years explored here, 1970-1976, have been characterized by certain streams of social development and change which appear to have had considerable intervening effect upon the relationship between society and the individual family. It would be unrealistic to consider this period without particular reference to changes in female roles, economic recession, and changes in matters related to birth control. Indeed, these matters have gained such prominence that they can be studied as societal outcomes in their own right, with indicators to provide measures of the rapidity of changes. Thus, some of these indicators, so closely intertwined with family behavior, are introduced as characteristics of society with particular impact upon family life.

FEMALE ROLE CHANGE

• The National Institute of Mental Health commissioned five national surveys between 1964 and 1974, which were summarized as follows:

> Between 1964 and 1974 women of all ages throughout the country became more "liberated" in the way they saw themselves in relation to men, marriage, children and work. The rising egalitarian spirit took hold in a wide range of women, not just the educated middle-class women who are most outspoken about feminist issues.[2]

• Participation by women in the labor force increased 68 percent in the period 1940 to 1973.[3]
• Between 1950 and 1975, there was a three-fold increase in the number of women who sought work and who had husbands in the home and children under the age of six.[4]
• A 1974 national survey by the Institute of Life Insurance found

that only about one in four young women intended to spend little or no time working during her lifetime. It may be concluded, therefore, that women's labor force participation rates will continue to expand for some time to come.[5]

• The Institute of Life Insurance concludes, "Since the mid- sixties the proportion of men of college age attending college has dropped somewhat, while the proportion of women of college age attending college has steadily increased."[6] This statistic allows the Institute to project that approximately the same proportion of women as men between the ages of 25 and 29 will have a college degree by 1980.

The trend toward egalitarianism in attitudes, employment, and education appears to be a rapidly developing movement which must affect behaviors within marital, parental, and other familial roles. The change is heralded by a series of organized structures that both politicize and support the change emotionally. New laws and new administration of old laws undergird a massive shift in the assumptions held about males and females. It appears that this shift will have a profound effect upon the institution of the family, and that it will be a long-developing trend.

ECONOMIC RECESSION

• From 1970 to 1976 the economic conditions were marked by recessionary trends and may have profound effects on the family. The economy now seems to be going through a fairly sluggish period marked by considerable unemployment, even during spurts of recovery.

• A national survey of 1,247 families made in midwinter 1974–75 indicated that American families have decreasing confidence in the economic future. Forty-five percent of the sample "have begun to accept the idea that each year may not be better financially." This finding would appear to debunk the American myth of endless economic betterment. The survey also indicated that 53 percent felt insecure about their own long-range economic future.[7] Moreover, at the time of the survey, 37 percent of American families were feeling "real economic stress." They report that their standard of living is lower than a year ago and their previous way of life is in jeopardy.[8] The period has been characterized not only by objective indicators of recession, but also by deep-seated changes in attitude since the longer periods of prosperity prior to 1970.

BIRTH CONTROL

A technology for easy birth control coupled with rapid changes in popular ethics produced a situation of rapid change in fertility between 1970 and 1976, which more freqently was planned rather than simply a matter of chance. Major changes were taking place in family fertility and an element of choice had entered the picture.

• A long-term trend toward a decreasing birth rate was evidenced by the fact that the 1975 birth rate was only 76 percent of that in 1965 and 49 percent of that in 1910.[9]
• In 1975, the Metropolitan Life Insurance Company made a series of projections based upon expected birth rates for various age groups using one method for 1960, 1965,and 1970, and a second method to repeat the activity for 1967 and 1972. In both instances, the trends toward birth rates significantly below expectations held up.[10]
• However, as recently as the period 1965–70, 13 percent of white births and 27 percent of black births had been unwanted.[11] With the birth control technology available at that time, it would appear that there was still room for a considerable decrease in the fertility rates by proper use of birth control methods.
• More recently, court decisions made it possible to control birth through abortion. "Women are increasingly electing to interrupt their pregnancies. Before the liberalization of abortion laws, legal abortions averaged approximately two per 1,000 births. By 1973, there were 239 legal abortions for each 1,000 live births. In the short period between 1970 and 1974, there was almost a five-fold increase in the number of legal abortions reported."[12]

During this period, a complex array of choices related to fertility faced both the unmarried and the married. Options never before available regarding the taking on of parental responsibilities became a common aspect of decision making for American adults. Accompanying normative changes which tended to condone family planning meant that the decisions were less couched within a framework of clear community sanctions.

Thus, Americans moved into a period of considerable uncertainty about aspects of themselves and their intimate relations with others. Clarity about the function of oneself as a male or as a female, about the "naturalness" of parenthood, and about improving economic supports over the long term had been made subject to question by political, social, economic, and technological developments which were ultimately social in origin. In effect, social sanctions (and certainties) had been replaced by socially supported alternatives which could be adopted with a freedom never before available within a context so open that marriage and the family itself could virtually be an experiment.[13]

Within this broad context of social change the indicator data relating to the family's response to modern society are approached. Demographic data about the family are available in greater profusion than are survey data. Such information is collected frequently through the census and census surveys. Furthermore, it is readily measurable, as the census is essentially a counting device. The emphasis in such data is upon *structure* rather than the quality of life.

WHAT HAS BEEN HAPPENING TO FAMILY STRUCTURE?

In considering what has been happening to the structure of the family, the data tend to cluster around what appear to be significant developments during the period. The major divisions for that arrangement of the indicators utilized here include data concerning traditional marriage and the family, divorce and separation, single-parent families, reconstituted families, and alternate forms of family living.

TRADITIONAL MARRIAGE

Clearly, there has been a depression in marriage rates. It is possible, however, that marriage is being delayed rather than abandoned. Young people may simply be postponing marriage because they cannot afford it during an economic recession. Furthermore, with wider birth control and abortion, it is possible that "forced" marriages have been eliminated to a considerable extent, thus slowing the marriage rate. Marriage may be valued so highly that it may be entered into with greater care (and more experimentation) than when taken more lightly. It may be less a symbolic entry into the adult world and more a considered optional action. Conversely, it is possible that marriage is becoming less popular, that alternatives to marriage are increasingly chosen as lifestyles in preference to marriage. A more detailed look at the data, while producing no conclusive results, may deepen the discussion.

• There has been an absolute numerical decrease in marriages over the past several years.[14]

• Jessie Bernard compared the years 1970 and 1974 as to changes in marital status. She found a significant decrease in the percentage of married men and women in most age groups and an increase in the percentage of divorced, separated, and single persons.[15]

• The United States Census has reported an increase in the *proportion* of single-person households from 13.1 percent in 1960 to 19.6 percent in 1975.[16]

• Between 1970 and 1975, census data indicated that the number of persons aged 25 to 34 who had never married increased by some 50 percent. Further data from the same source indicated that, in the period 1960 to 1975, in the 20 to 24 age range, the number of single women increased from 28 to 40 percent, and single men from 53 to 60 percent.[17]

• There is good reason, however, to doubt that these data truly indicate a lessening interest in marriage. Paul Glick particularly examined what has happened to women in the 35 to 44 age range and found a continuing decrease in the percentages of those living in a single state.[18]

• Recent history would suggest that age at first marriage is increasing. For men, the median age at first marriage rose from 22.8 in 1960 to 23.5 in 1975. For women, the increase was from 20.3 to 21.2.[19]

• A national opinion survey conducted in 1974 indicated that an overwhelming majority felt positively toward marriage, while only 14 percent indicated attitudes that were basically negative toward themselves or others becoming married.[20]

In summary, traditional marriage is undergoing some changes. The bulk of evidence would suggest that marriages are being delayed, but, despite a numerical and proportional increase in adults living singly, it is likely that most people will continue to be married in their lifetimes, although possibly at older ages. It remains uncertain whether the trend will continue. The origin is recent, the causes obscure, and the meaning uncertain. Present data, although mixed, suggest not only a continuing need to watch demographic studies, but also a need to develop attitudinal data which would indicate the degree to which traditional marriage is going out of favor.

DIVORCE AND SEPARATION

Indicators concerned with divorce and separation are the most dramatic of all. The data are so clear that the conclusion is that divorce is increasing at a remarkable pace in the United States.

• In the period between 1920 and 1975, the number of divorced women increased sixfold. In the past hundred years, 1875 to 1975, there has been a sixteenfold increase in the divorce rate.[21]
• By 1971, the divorce rate in the United States was the highest among populous nations throughout the world, with the rate increasing in subsequent years.[22]
• The class characteristics of those divorcing have been changing. Divorce was once associated with lower class status, but the trend now seems to be toward "democratization" as divorce spreads throughout the entire U.S. population.[23]
• Another trend seems to be receding. Earlier data suggested that those who divorced remarried, thus implying a continued faith in marriage as an appropriate lifestyle even though adults experienced failure in marriage. Between the mid-1950s and 1973, however, the divorce rate had increased by two-thirds, whereas the remarriage rate of those divorced had increased by only one-third.[24] In fact, between 1970 and 1975, the proportion of di-

vorced who had not remarried had increased from seven to ten percent.[25]

• Although their sample was hardly scientifically chosen, there was an indication of another trend change in the observations of Tracers Company of America, a firm specializing in locating deserting spouses. The offhand statement was that whereas in 1965 the odds of a woman deserting a man were 300 to one, by 1973 the two sexes were even in desertion patterns, and in 1974 there were more women than men who were deserting.[26]

• Perhaps the most poignant statistic on divorce concerns the children who are affected. In the period between 1953 and 1971, the number of children of divorced parents tripled.[27]

SINGLE-PARENT FAMILIES

As might be expected from the divorce statistics, there has also been a dramatic rise in the number of women raising children in households without a husband present. The emphasis here is on female-headed households, still the primary statistical group making up single-parent families in the United States.

• By 1975, 15 percent of all families were headed by women, a rise from 9 percent in 1960.[28] This 15 percent represented a very sizable proportion of families in which children were being raised, and the fact requires some reorientation to the plight of the single-parent family. Often, such families have been seen as statistically deviant at least, and pathological at most. Considering that these families are often so constituted only temporarily because of remarriage their proportion is all the more significant, suggesting that some family experience in a single-parent family is common enough to be considered a norm in the United States.

• Between 1960 and 1973, there was a 47 percent rise in the proportion of all American families headed by women.[29]

• The tie with divorce becomes clear in considering the statistic that 50.6 percent of divorced women continued to function as parents in 1974—an increase from 46.2 percent in 1970.[30]

• The Bureau of the Census presents statistics on female-headed households up to 1973. (Table 1.)

•Between 1970 and 1975, there was a 45 percent increase in the

TABLE 1

FEMALE PRIMARY INDIVIDUALS AS PROPORTION OF ALL HOUSEHOLD HEADS 1973, 1970, AND 1960

(Numbers in thousands)

Type of unit and sex of head	1973	1970	1960	Increase 1970-73	Increase 1960-70	% Increase 1970-73	% Increase 1960-70
All household heads	68,251	63,573	52,809	4,678	10,764	7.4	20.4
Female primary individuals	8,858	7,801	4,979	1,057	2,822	13.5	56.7
Precent of all heads	13.0	12.3	9.4	(X)	(X)	(X)	(X)
Living alone	8,239	7,150	4,436	1,089	2,714	15.2	61.2
Percent of female primary individuals	93.0	91.7	89.1	(X)	(X)	(X)	(X)

From: *Female Family Heads* (Washington, D.C.: U.S. Government Printing Office 1974, Series P-23, no. 50, p. 28.

number of children living with their single-parent mother. By 1975, 20 percent of all children were either living with single parents or were being cared for by those not their parents.[31]

• The number of female-headed families is huge. In 1970, there were 5.6 million. By 1975, there were 7.2 million.[32]

• Black families have a much higher proportion of female heads than do white families. (Table 2.)

• The growth rate of these families, as compared with husband-wife families with children, is extremely dramatic. (Chart I indicates this comparison.)

TABLE 2

PERCENTAGES OF FEMALE HEADS OF FAMILIES BY RACE AND AGE, 197?

	20-24	25-29	30-34	35-39	40-44
White	3.5	6.7	8.0	9.9	9.1
Negro	16.4	28.1	32.6	32.1	32.2

From: Jessie Bernard, Notes on Changing Lifestyles, *Journal of Marriage and the Family,* August 1975, p. 585.

CHART I
GROWTH RATE OF FEMALE-HEADED FAMILIES WITH CHILDREN, 1950 TO 1974

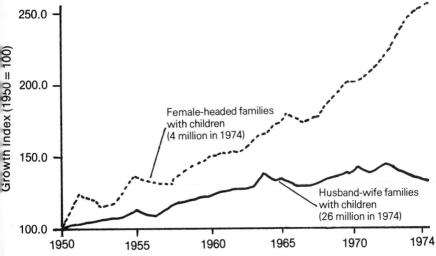

From: Heather L. Ross and Isabel V. Sawhill, *Time of Transition: The Growth of Families Headed by Women* (Washington, D.C.: The Urban Institute, 1975), Figure 1, p. 2. Reprinted by permission of the Urban Institute.

Several inferences can clearly be drawn from these data. The rise in recent years of single-parent families headed by women is phenomenal. This family form has attained a kind of normalcy in the United States unimaginable fifteen years ago. The phenomenon has a decided racial character, being particularly common among blacks. This fact is prominent enough to be associated with a literature of debate, centering on the black family experience, which is well beyond the purview of this writing.[33] However, the proportion of these families in the United States is now high enough to affect the very character of the American family experience.

RECONSTITUTED FAMILIES

Remarkably little attention has been given to another outgrowth of the increasingly temporary quality of American marriages.

• In 1975, census figures indicated that 80 percent of those divorced remarried.[34] With the rising rates of divorce, this statistic meant that there was a significant portion of the family population which had been reconstituted from an earlier family form.

• A large portion of the child population is living in such families. In 1970, more than 30 percent of the children under 18 in the United States were not living with both natural parents.[35]

The nature and quality of these reconstituted families have rarely been studied, but some data exist which use self ratings of satisfaction in marriages following earlier marriages.

• A very small study by Lucille Duberman suggests reason for optimism in the capacities of reconstituted families to meet their own ideals.[36]

• Several surveys of the Institute of Social Research at the University of Michigan yield results with greater face validity than the Duberman study. Angus Campbell, *et al.*, developed a system for scoring the respondents' assessment of their relationship with their spouse. Their findings suggest that reconstituted families include marriages which are assessed by the partners positively, in fact slightly more so than first marriages.[37] It is notable that use of the same scale yields very negative ratings for marital partners who are currently divorced or separated. Admittedly these data are crude, but they do begin to suggest that there is some reason for optimism about the viability of family experience despite high rates of divorce.

Much more needs to be learned about the experience of children involved in temporary marriages, single-parent experiences, and reconstituted families. There is little available social indicator information on the subject, which has usually been studied from the viewpoint of pathology. Correlations between family disturbance and pathological behavior can be demonstrated; however, other factors can be correlated similarly with social pathology. It is possible to surmise that a substantial minority of Americans experience marriage and the family increasingly as a temporary state; that marriage, with increasing frequency, is a serial matter; and that reconstituted families can be successful. But social indicators to date reveal surprisingly little about the meaning to children affected by, and involved with, these choices which are primarily made by adults.

ALTERNATE FORMS

Thus far, traditional marriage and what has been happening to it has been considered. Another perspective is useful: What is happening to family forms that are direct challenges to the traditional family as characterized by celebrated marriage and legitimate children?

There is no question that the form of the family is being challenged by an increasingly substantial minority. At the same time, the traditional marriage is undergoing some major shifts in purpose as marital partners reconsider the raising of children, considering this course more of an option than ever before. The childless marriage is considered an alternate form of family here because it so clearly reconstitutes the nature of family life.

• "The average household has shrunk in size from five persons in 1910 to less than three persons in 1975."[38] Thus, the United States has long shown a trend toward smaller families.
• This trend has accelerated recently, and by 1973 the United States birthrate was the lowest in its history, arriving at a point of zero population growth.[39]
• In 1960, the number of live births was slightly more than 4.2 million. In 1974, it had declined to about 3.1 million.[40]
• By 1974, the goal of a small family, related to population reproduction at the rate of zero population growth, seemed well established in the child-bearing population and was coupled with a trend toward a willingness to postpone the birth of children through birth control methods.[41]
• By 1974, a major national survey of young women between the ages of 14 and 25 indicated a striking 86 percent acceptance overall of childless marriage.[42] In effect, not only were births decreasing, but a childless lifestyle was apparently being accepted as a permissible norm by an overwhelming majority of the young.

Perhaps even more remarkable was the change in attitude toward men and women living together without legal marriage procedure.

• During the 1960s, census figures indicated an eight-fold increase in nonrelatives living together.[43]

• The trend continued into the 1970s. The previously married were included in the change. Between 1970 and 1974, the United States experienced a 21.5 percent increase in the number of divorced women who chose to live with nonrelatives rather than remarry.[44]

• Children were clearly involved as a result of these changes, despite the lowering birth rate. "The proportion of births that occurred outside of marriage more than tripled between 1950 and 1974."[45]

• Harold Edrich cites several opinion surveys concerning alternative lifestyles which compare fairly radical choices with those not considered so. The findings of these surveys suggest that radical alternatives are relatively unpopular, and many who would approve them would not themselves act accordingly. In fact, the degree of conservatism is striking. However, a significant minority either strongly or moderately approve, or consider themselves at least somewhat likely to adopt alternative lifestyles.[46]

• Edrich has also gathered survey data indicating a marked increase from 1972 to 1973 among the young in general approval of the idea of communal living.[47] Because the data describe only a one- year period and are based on a relatively small national sample, there is reason to doubt that opinion is shifting so quickly. Nevertheless, once again there is an indication of change in the direction of radical forms of living.

The temporal component in alternate family forms is extremely important. It is one thing for a population to postpone births and diminish family size; quite another for it to dismiss parenthood. It is one thing for the young to live together for emotional, sexual, and financial convenience predating their marriages; quite another for them to choose temporary liaisons as being preferable to marriage. It is one thing for a divorced person to choose some form of communal living to ease the transition between marriages and to arrange for easy care of children; quite another to prefer communal living over marital pairing for sexual fulfillment. The data cited tell us little about how these alternatives are chosen. What is known is that major shifts are taking place in the choices that are being made.

It is important to remember that aged couples living together as a financial convenience are contained within the data concerning alternate family forms. Young couples without adequate employment opportunities are contained within the zero population group figures. Family forms reveal little about the attitudes behind the choices made, or circumstances that shift the weight of economically rational choices made by many families. Communes may be primarily based on baby-sitting arrangements, or they may be radical group marriages. Divorces may be expressions of contempt for permanence or wishes for greater commitment than is available. Clearly, family structure is in the process of changing in a massive way. What is needed now are data to help us in understanding the *quality* of the change and thus its meaning. But, to understand changes in structure it is also necessary to understand what is happening to family functions.

WHAT IS HAPPENING TO THE FUNCTIONS OF THE FAMILY?

To understand what is happening to family functions social indicators which are more oblique, or where the data are much thinner must be used. In the United States, structural changes in family patterns tend to be monitored more successfully than functional descriptions, which can lead to a greater sense of the quality of family life. Social indicators concerning family structure have been used continually to describe disturbance in the family. It is notable that little progress has been made in the development of more qualitative indicators. Data cited concerning family functions may be readily characterized as less direct, and more challengeable. Samples are smaller, and questions can often be raised as to whether the results cited are actually pertinent to the functional capacity of families.

EXPRESSION AND AFFECTION

• In a large national survey of 2502 families, the most highly rated personal values expressed were related to family life.[48]

• In another larger survey, 90 percent of a nationwide sample of 1000 adult males and 3000 adult females stressed love and communication as the most important elements in a good marriage.[49]

• The Campbell, studies have demonstrated from their poll of 2074 adults that satisfaction derived from marital experience is a key to the satisfaction adults feel with family life as a whole; that the quality of marriage is a predictor of the satisfaction felt with family life.[50] These investigators also found that family satisfaction is the highest predictor of general well-being experienced by individuals.[51]

• It is clear that most adults find real satisfaction with family life. The Campbell studies show 94 percent of women and 96 percent of men reporting that their role as parents has at least usually been enjoyable.[52]

• Another large-sample poll from the mid-1970s shows similarly positive responses from those engaged in family experience; 78 percent of those polled expressed a sense of satisfaction with the way the family worked together on family finances.[53]

In summary, the limited data available suggest that the affectional and expressive function of the family continues to be meaningful to adults living within a family. Emotional satisfaction is rated highly as a reason for marriage, and those who are married seem to experience a great deal of satisfaction. Even specific aspects of interpersonal relationships within the family seem to test out well as being satisfying. Affection and expression seem to be real aspects of American family experience, and they are valued highly both as reasons for the family to exist and as components of a sense of individual well-being.

SOCIALIZATION AND ENCULTURATION

The socialization and enculturation process, primarily as expressed through the influence of parents and the family upon children, has not been measured directly. However, it is possible to examine some factors which bear a likely relationship with the function itself.

• An opinion research survey of 1522 women in a representative national sample published in 1975 indicates a trend toward egalitarianism between the roles of mother and father, as the young perceive them.[54] Apparently the socialization process is becoming less a perceived responsibility of women and more a combined and shared parental function for both partners.

Although data from organized programs have weaknesses as social indicators, national trends in the provision of foster care outside the family household are increasing at too rapid a pace to be ignored. Despite the fact that the figures are in many ways a reflection of budgetary priorities within governments, more families are turning to government resources to function as a substitute for child care within the family.

• According to United States government figures, in 1960 there were 241,900 children cared for by some kind of foster care. By 1971, the figure had risen to 330,373,[55] an increase of 37 percent.

• However, child care outside the home is not usually a foster care situation. A study of 1207 families with working mothers of children under 12 indicated a much more varied pattern of child care, with the head of the family taking an active role in making personal arrangements for care facilities.[56] (Table 3.)

An interesting point is that modes of child care which would appear to involve the parents and family seem to be preferred over more institutionalized forms of care where parents might be less directly involved in the supervision. If socialization and en-culturation occur outside the family setting, parents seem to opt for some kind of continuing role or control of the process.

• With all the external care arrangements, the family continues to function in the socialization and enculturation process. Gisela Konopka's study of adolescent girls indicates that her respondents have experienced reasonable limitations in their lives, have taken on responsibilities which are related to family needs, and see pur-posiveness in the demands placed upon them by the family.[57] Konopka concludes from her in-depth interviews with a small national sample that a very active process is occurring between parents and children, and she argues against what she conceives to be the myth of permissiveness in American child care.

TABLE 3

MODE OF CHILD CARE

Day care, nursery	8.0%	Relatives not living with family	17.4%
Sitter, friend	24.2%	Take care of selves	2.0%
Head or wife	23.9%	Public school	10.7%
Relatives living with family	9.8%	Other, unspecified	3.9%

From: Jessie Bernard, Notes on Changing Lifestyles, *Journal of Marriage and the Family*, August 1975, p.585.

Even more compelling is a study by Yankelovich, Skelly, and White, Inc. which utilizes a large representative national sample of parents and children to survey parent-child relationships.[58] The study develops a sizable profile of the nature of values that parents attempt to transmit to their children, also indicating that the process is one of high priority to parents; yet there are indications that the nature of the profile is changing. There has developed a profound difference between a "new breed" of parents, who encourage self-actualization, and the more traditional, who are more authoritarian in approach. Furthermore, children reflect aspects of these differences in parental behavior.

One might conclude from these data that the trend toward having both parents work outside the home has led families to search for outside supports for child care. There does seem to be an increasing group of "casualties"—children who are turned over to foster care when families are unable to provide. But less drastic departures from care within the family itself are used to an increasing extent and seem to be chosen when they provide some degree of control and interaction on the parents' part. Moreover, children still show that they are deeply affected by the socialization and enculturation process within the family. A social indicator approach tends to support the depth of influence the family carries, as do the less systemized observations of clinicians, who have for some time seen a strong connection between serious personality problems and troubled family experience. Socialization and enculturation as family functions have certainly been modified and perhaps even weakened, but the functions do continue and there are indications that parents actively seek to maintain them.

CONTINUITY

The ties among immediate family members, or the sense of intergenerational connection, provides an important index of the way in which the family functions as a source of continuity for individuals.

• The Konopka study indicates that adolescents feel closest to those adults who are family members: their parents and their grandparents.[59] In effect, these data point toward intergenerational ties.

• Barbara Bryant, *et al.*, asked a national sample of 1005 women, "How certain do you feel that your marriage will last until you or your husband dies?" Ninety-four percent of the respondents were at least fairly certain, and 75 percent were absolutely certain. The responses remained fairly parallel across age groups.[60]

• Campbell, *et al.*, polled a national sample of 2164 adults regarding their sense of closeness to their living parents. The poll demonstrated that these adults had retained close relationships with their parents, and only a small minority felt less close than what they considered to be "average" in all families.[61]

Although the foregoing indicate that there are affective ties between members of nuclear as well as extended families, there is a question about the degree to which these ties have functional purpose. One such concern has to do with the care of the young and the old, and whether the extended family plays a part.

• Katherine Dickinson has surveyed the process by which care services for children are paid. She finds that nearly one-half of working mothers do not pay for child care expenses and that most of the costs are borne by other members of the nuclear and extended family.[62]

• Through the population census it is possible to examine trends in the use of the extended family in caring for the elderly. There was a marked decrease between 1960 and 1970, the percentage of elderly with extended family members decreasing from 37 to 30 percent.[63] This indicator is difficult to interpret because such intervening variables as newly available facilities for the aged and changes in morbidity and mortality rates might be the actual sources of shifts in care plans.

A continuing tie among family members, extended to intergenerational linkages, can be demonstrated by social indicators. Most of the indicators suggest rather strong linkages between family members, and the expectation that these will continue over time. However, there seems to be a decrease in the use of the extended family as a care resource for the aged.

INTERACTION WITH THE ENVIRONMENT

Indicators that explain how individuals interact through the family with the environment are virtually nonexistent. The matter has been most frequently approached in literature concerning socioeconomic deprivation, with particular reference to minority groups. The result is that an overall picture of the family and the ways in which an exchange occurs between the individual and society by means of family resources remain uncertain. So also does the nature of change in this function within the family. Yet the matter remains important, not only as a means of diagnosing what is occurring within the family, but also as a means of understanding socioeconomic mobility and the factors required to support this American ideal.

CONSUMPTION

There are also problems about data related to the family as consumer. Marketing research tends to be focused too narrowly on individual goods to offer general conclusions. Some data are concerned broadly with family attitudes toward money, and an examination of them serves as an oblique means of inferring how the family functions as a consumer.

• A poll of 1247 families in a national sample indicates that husbands and wives agree upon the state of family finances.[64] It can therefore be surmised that an active process of evaluation occurs between spouses in regard to consumption capability.

• The data are somewhat confusing concerning family self-evaluations of money management. Ninety-one percent of the families surveyed indicated that they felt that their family managed finances well.[65]

• Nevertheless, 63 percent criticized the way in which their family handled money in the previous year.[66] This statistic might suggest that families gauge their responses to survey questions with considerable discretion. Within a global positive rating, families can still be self-critical and find room for improvement.

• Eighty percent of families in one poll reported that they talked enough or too much about money,[67] again showing the high priority money matters get in family interactions.

• The great majority of parents, 73 percent overall, involve their children in money matters and do so increasingly as the children grow older.[68] There is an active process of enculturation into the world of consumption and finance.

• When family members polled were asked about who sacrificed need satisfaction to meet family consumption patterns, there was a surprising feeling of equality. Eighty-six percent felt that all members of the family shared equally in making a sacrifice.[69]

All these data suggest that the family functions as a consumer, does so through involving all family members, and puts high priority on this function. It is surprising that such an apparently central force in the nation's consumption patterns is so poorly understood with reference to the question of increasing or decreasing function over time. Even with the lack of time series data, however, it can be inferred that the consumption function is strong and relatively unscathed by some of the social factors that raise question about other family functions. The culture would appear to support the family's involvement with consumption, even when it may thwart its desired level of consumption.

The social indicators cited in this chapter are derived from many different sources. Chief among them is the U.S. Census Bureau, whose focus is demographic and descriptive and whose surveys are either population-wide or very large, carefully designed representative samples. The remainder of the data comes largely from polls, the quality of which varies considerably. An overview of data available reveals that survey data are much less developed than demographic studies. There is a clear need for greater centrality in the process of collecting social indicators concerning the family, possibly a national bureau concerned specifically with family research.

IMPRESSIONISTIC PROFILE OF THE AMERICAN FAMILY

From the social indicators now available, an impressionistic profile of the American family in the mid-1970s emerges—something of a composite picture of family life.

• Women, married or not, are becoming full participants in the job market. This pervasive fact clearly affects other findings.

• The young are having fewer children. It appears that they are exercising choice in whether to have children, and this choice may be affected by the current economic recession. Thus, it is unclear whether the continued decreasing birth rate is temporary, or whether a basic change in attitude toward having children is being expressed.

• Marriage is occurring at the end of a longer, more complex period of deliberating choices. Marriage may often be preceded by a temporary arrangement of "living together" in some "marital" form. Furthermore, some young people seem to be making a choice not to marry, in numbers that suggest that the process of choosing is more active than it has been in years past.

• Exercising the right to make a choice also includes the possibility of divorcing if a marriage is not satisfactory. Moreover, remarrying after divorce is more frequently a matter of choosing among options, and a significant minority of the divorced either remain single or decide to live together without marriage. It is notable, however, that when the divorced do remarry, there are indications that adjustments are made rather well.

• Because of the increase in divorce, there has been an enormous rise in the number of female-headed families, many of which contain children. This family form is approaching a norm for the raising of children in the United States. A very large minority of children experience living without one parent, usually the father, at some time before they are grown up.

• Among the married, it seems less clear that it is necessary to have children. Childless couples are becoming more common. Opinions suggest that marriage need not be child-centered and the matter of having children is an open option. In fact, more radical alternatives in lifestyle are gradually becoming more frequently accepted by the population at large.

But despite these changes (or perhaps because so many choices are now available) families continue to rate highly as sources of personal satisfaction for individuals.

• Most parents enjoy their children, and both males and females are moving toward equivalent participation in their upbringing.
• Although children are more frequently being provided with physical care outside the home, it is apparent that parents are tending to resist a loss of influence upon those care arrangements. They make choices permitting them to retain a degree of control of the caretakers. The continuing impact of the family and parents upon children remains apparent despite these trends toward outside care.
• Although divorce is increasing, attitudes toward marriage continue to be connected with permanence. People marry expecting their marriages to last throughout their lifetimes.
• The influence of extended families continues. Often, extended family members influence family functions on several fronts. One area where the extended family has seemed to be losing influence is in the care of the aged, who have often turned away (or been turned away) from the extended family as a resource.
• Family decisions seem to influence the behavior of individuals in society generally. The family continues to be a primary source of socialization.

Thus, a global impression of the family today, reveals a picture of fairly traditional attitudes being expressed through choices which may support them, but which are less rigidly defined along lines of sexual morals, sex-roles, or single-pattern processes of caring for children throughout their minority. Americans seem to be demanding that their families function and, when they don't, they are increasingly willing to make radical life changes.

SHORTCOMINGS OF CURRENT KNOWLEDGE

It is indeed ominous that massive changes are occurring in the structure of so basic a social institution as the family with so little concerted effort to understand the meaning behind these changes. The fabric of American life appears to be intimately connected with the family, yet there are notable gaps in knowledge of what is happening to families.

1. **A lack of understanding of the nature of lifestyle choices.** Virtually nothing is known about what is involved in the process of choosing a particular lifestyle. What incentives are at work? Are large numbers making a choice against formal families, or only seeking temporary alternatives for convenience?

2. **Inadequate information about reconstituted families.** Little is known of the effects of major change in family structure on those who cannot control the process—usually the children. Despite common wisdom, there is little information about the effects of family breakup on children. The population of reconstituted families has rarely been sampled, despite the prevalence of this family form.

3. **Incomplete knowledge of the single-parent family experience.** Now that it is clear that this family form is beginning to approach the traditional family in numbers and that such families often include the least affluent of American familes, the nature of the experience, and the ways social exchanges affect these families become of greatly increased importance.

4. **Confusion about how the family compares with other group experiences.** Studies might be designed to understand the competing impacts on individuals of various social organizations, as compared with the family.

5. **Inadequate knowledge of the place of the family in aiding individuals to function within society.** The social utility of the family in this sense is not clearly demonstrated.

Increasing knowledge in these areas requires much more than the fairly casual, often isolated questioning now inserted in public opinion polls. Continuity, a context of questions directed specifically to family life quality, and survey schedules that provide greater tests of internal validity, all will be necessary to begin to gain a real understanding of *the quality of family life.*

chapter 3

COLLECTIVITIES IN THE FAMILY POLICYMAKING ENVIRONMENT

Government policymaking takes place not in a vacuum but within a framework of organizational interests and power relationships. The dynamic interactions that lead to policymaking have been described by Charles Lindblom as the "play of power."[1] Examination of the organizational process concerned with the family in the United States requires a foundation upon which to construct an analysis. What follows borrows heavily from the Lindblom model, assuming as it does that the process by which policy is made consists of organizational interests; that these interests are in dynamic interaction; and that organizations differ in their proximity to policymaking.

At the same time, the analysis that is presented also represents a considerable departure from the Lindblom model. The position here is that proximate policymakers (using Lindblom's term) are not yet active in developing cohesive, comprehensive policy in regard to the American family. Consequently, there is not yet organized cooperation among proximate policymakers, and the rules for interest group behavior in influencing policymaking, which Lindblom describes, have not yet been formulated. Whatever family policy has emerged has been implicit in a series of program emphases, and there has been only oblique interest in the effect of policy upon the family. Apparently, the Lindblom process has been otherwise engaged—unless the problems of making policy for the family have led to unwitting collusion in avoiding the subject! The underlying assumption here is that explicit policymaking for the American family is underdeveloped and that organizational mapping provides insight into why such policymaking has moved so slowly in the United States.

FAMILIES AS INTEREST GROUPS

Families themselves have had remarkably little to say about policy related to family life. Yet, families are not inherently incapable of organizing to affect policy. Many European nations have formed grass roots family unions that have had important policy effects, establishing constituencies for policymakers interested in the welfare of families.[2]

Family life in the United States is pluralistic to a far greater extent than it is in the European nations that have succeeded in evolving effective family coalitions. It is difficult for families with radically differing lifestyles to perceive common cause among themselves, or to understand what might be involved in comprehensive political activity concerning all families. The problem of diversity is described in an excerpt from an article discussing ethnic groups.

> Further, the middle class family model is not a viable tool for the assessment of extended or partially extended systems. The range of family orientations is as varied as the ethnic groups themselves, and no one working assessment model can apply. . . that no one model is more American than another, in that the ethnic phenomenon originated in this society and is thus a product of this society.[3]

This well-established phenomenon of ethnicity in American society (despite the melting pot myth), and the diversity of lifestyles accompanying it may well be a subtle support for the growing pluralism of forms of family life that social indicators evidence. Pluralistic patterns, whether based on ethnic groups or on new options, determined or freely chosen, can be demonstrated to be a central part of the American social fabric. Nations with less diversity may more easily coalesce around common principles.

A second major cultural deterrent to family activity in policy development for families may be what David and Vera Mace have identified as the "inter-marital taboo"; married persons are not expected to discuss their personal lives easily outside the family circle. The Maces describe socially determined constraints upon such communication as threatening status, initiating anxieties about potential sexual conquest of a dissatisfied partner, challenging cultural taboos against explicit discussion of sexuality, or threatening the closed boundaries of the family. They decry these constraints upon communication as self-defeating, and urge greater sharing of problems across family lines.[4]

It may well be that data exemplified by the indicators in Chapter 2, which suggest high idealism accompanied by decreasing capacity to meet these ideals, may leave those whose families' lives are problematic ashamed of their performance and unable to freely communicate their feeling. There also seems to be little general knowledge of the dynamics of family failure. The result may be difficulty in engaging in a coalitional process, particularly regarding realistic problems, because communication is so severely blocked.

In the United States, no widespread family movement has entered the policy arena with great strength. Direct family experience has not been enlisted in any meaningful way in developing a constituency of families, and it would appear that such a coalition could not be established around a singular set of norms regarding the definition of family, or valued family behavior. Rather more sophisticated appreciation of pluralism as a principle would be required in order to engage families across barriers of cultural difference in the United States.

FAMILY-ORIENTED GROUPS

It is surprising that with the numerous governmental programs concerned with human needs, central interest in the family as such has never characterized any federal bureau. The Children's Bureau and the Office of Child Development, although frequently concerned with the effects of family life upon children, have tended to see the family as a resource for the child rather than as an object of attention in its own right. Within the U.S. Department of Health, Education, and Welfare, the Division of Family Services became so named at the time the Family

Assistance Plan legislation was developed; it is simply another name for the welfare system. Although this Division may be conceived to be family-centered, it is questionable that it is a programmatic expression of a central policy committed to the American family,[5] and American welfare policies have even been described as antifamilial.[6]

Moreover, federal agencies have tended to be concerned with policy for carrying out programs, not policies as contexts for program development in the family area. (This difference as central in the formation of family policy, as well as federal avoidance of policymaking for families, with family law and policy passed to state authority will be discussed later in this book.)

To date, there has been little for family advocates to rally around with reference to government, but there has been a set of organized interest groups developed around familial matters, some of recent and some of older origin. It is these groups that are characterized as "family-oriented groups." They have not accumulated power in policy arenas and they have found it difficult to coalesce.

There are several possibilities for formulating interest in the family, and multiple interests have been expressed in the formation of organizations. In general, the emphasis has been to *do* something rather than to form around a principle for policymaking. As family problems have been perceived in society, programs have been developed to educate families, to provide social services for them, to develop skilled professional groups capable of counseling them, to study them, or to organize them into participatory groups. Policy has developed implicitly, not explicitly. These programmatic themes tend to be somewhat mixed in practice. Organizations borrow from each other or reinvent concepts of service which may overlap even as they modify. It is possible, however, to trace organizational development regarding the family in the United States with reference to the general programmatic emphases described above.

HOME ECONOMICS

The late nineteenth century was a period of great expansion of interest in social problems. Beginning with the period of the Civil War, social reformers made themselves heard in the United

States. The times brought particular attention to the poor, who seemed to be multiplying, particularly with the waves of immigration the United States was experiencing. There were early concerns with health and well-being which came to be differentiated into discrete movements. One of these was the home economics movement, which grew out of a concern that the skills of the poor were inadequate for proper home maintenance. The home economics field tended to move into an *educational* design to aid in handling family consumption patterns and to help families use a more "scientific" approach.

The movement burgeoned and developed a number of specialties. By 1966, the American Home Economics Association (AHEA), which encompassed a constituency of both university departments in home economics which were accredited by the Association and the home economists themselves who were certified by it, had arrived at several goals including "encouraging and promoting wider and better understanding of the value of home economics to individuals and to nations; understanding of the significant place of homemaking in our society; cooperation with other community, national, and international groups concerned with family well-being; improvement of the standards of preparation and of continued professional growth of its members; application of the physical, biological, and social sciences and of the arts of homemaking; investigation and research important to the family and to the institutional household; and legislation designed to aid in the improvement of home and family life."[7]

A central concern was the application of scientific method to homemaking, and many of the specialized uses of home economists were directed to this concern. They were employed in high schools and colleges for purposes of educating homemakers, but they were also utilized in extension departments in urban and agricultural settings and had developed a foothold in the study of consumerism as it related to corporate enterprise.

As this field developed, home economics was expanded on many university campuses toward generic study of the family. It included treatment of the family and family life education as specialties, particularly on the doctoral level. Many of these sequences were interdisciplinary, responsive to the trend within the home economics field to utilize a broad range of disciplines to provide theory for education purposes.

SOCIAL SERVICES

Also in the latter part of the nineteenth century, the pioneer forerunners of modern voluntary social welfare organizations were formed. The charity organization movement, originally a means to organize a broad range of charities, gradually moved in the direction of family-oriented social work. Care services for children, often originating with orphanages, moved in the direction of voluntary child welfare services. These movements, which tended to develop along parallel lines, retained a cooperative quality throughout their history. What became family service agencies sometimes included child welfare services, so that in many communities there developed combined family and children's agencies. However, as national movements, they retain some distinctions.

The charity organization societies that became family service agencies formed a national voluntary organization in 1911, now the Family Service Association of America. Similarly, the child welfare agencies formed the Child Welfare League of America (CWLA) in 1920, but this national organization's membership differed in that it included public as well as private agencies and retained a closer relationship to government. (Acceptance of governmental responsibility for the care of children was expressed federally in the establishment of the Children's Bureau in 1912.)

The family service field had originated with a concern for financial and in-kind assistance to the poor. In 1919, the national organization reaffirmed and underlined its concern for the family itself.[8] Finally, with the development of public responsibility for financial assistance as expressed in the Social Security Act of 1935, family service agencies, having had a close relationship with the development of the profession of social work, became focused on the counseling of families in interpersonal difficulty.[9] By 1975, Patrick Riley was able to state that the service programs of the family service agency were basically directed toward family counseling, family advocacy, and family life education.[10]

The child welfare field had also utilized the social work profession as central in its operations. Its program concerns, however, were more focused on the direct care of children; focus on families tended to be ancillary. The standards of the Child Welfare League of America (CWLA) for providing social services to families are described in *Service to Children in Their Own Homes.*[11] This title is suggestive of the League's emphasis: that child welfare services may be *extended* beyond direct care to the relationship of the child to his own family. Services are defined as based on social casework similar to that provided by family agencies, although supplementary services, such as homemaker services, may also be utilized. Preventive services are differentiated from protective services according to the presumed motivation of parents; "preventive" service requires that the parents seek help with a recognized problem.[12]

Both voluntary child welfare agencies and family service agencies are usually supported by private federated fund-raising, as exemplified by the United Way, although all these fields have some relationship to government activities, often through the medium of the program contract. However, despite commonalities in auspices, history, and program elements, there is a clear division between the two fields. Family service emphasizes family interaction as a central concern; child welfare sees the family as an important resource for the child rather than a client group in itself. Family service programs are generally directed to total family interests; child welfare programs tend to be directed to substitute care of children, or the prevention of it. In this respect they differ significantly from the newer movements that have a focal interest in the family.

THE PROFESSIONAL MODEL

Home economics, family service, and child welfare are all associated with certain professional developments. This is inherent in home economics, but the field has maintained an eclectic attitude in its professional education. As previously stated, both family service and child welfare have a close association with the development of professional social work. But as professional groups, neither home economists nor social workers can claim exclusive concern for the family.

Many therapists, specializing in counseling families, have sought to distinguish family-oriented activity through professional organization. The effort has been to seek recognition, including certification and licensing, for activity geared to marriage and family counseling. "The American Association of Marriage Counselors (now the American Association of Marriage and Family Counselors), and the National Council on Family Relations have been notable in their leadership of the movement toward present legislation."[13] This movement was interdisciplinary, and when the former organization convened a national forum on the state licensing of marriage counselors, "participants included consultants from the fields of psychology, psychiatry, social work, law and pastoral counseling."[14] The approach is inclusive; describing a model for licensing, Meyer Elkin states:

> The committee feels that a master's degree in marriage counseling, social work, pastoral counseling, psychology, sociology of the family, or a closely allied field is adequate as a minimum requirement. It does not regard the doctorate degree as absolutely essential. With the present great need for professionally trained marriage and family counselors it is unrealistic to set the doctorate degree as a minimum requirement, particularly when the counselor's personality itself seems to play such an important part in the counseling experience and its effectiveness.[15]

This inclusiveness has set the American Association of Marriage and Family Counselors (AAMFC) apart from other professional groups which retain interest in the family area, providing both an opportunity for enlargement of its own membership and a barrier to cooperative activities with other professional groups. AAMFC has tended to be concerned primarily with professional regulation, although it also provides possibilities for a forum among its members.

Another eclectic organization, the National Council of Family Relations (NCFR), has primarily acted as a forum among those interested in the family, and has tended to emphasize academic interests along with those of therapists. Many of the professionals have moved in the direction of private practice, or an entrepreneur model for their activity, a substantial difference from the more institutionalized organization of the older fields concerned with the family.

THE ACADEMIC MODEL

On a number of university campuses, interdisciplinary centers have developed that have a primary interest in the family, but there is little uniformity among them. Some are derivations or extensions of home economics departments, often with primary concern for applied research, family therapy, and family life education. Others have been the offspring of university interests in sociology and emphasize basic theory-building and research. Still others have recently developed to express an interest in family policy, utilizing policy science as a core concept. These centers are newly emerging and have not yet coalesced to influence professional development, common theory development, or public policy.

THE PARTICIPATORY MODEL

With the movements discussed above, there has been a common thread; all have been closely associated with professional organizations. As with the older movements, the emphasis has been on program, not policy. A number of groups have developed which either are hostile to professional interests or feel that there is a special place for participatory small groups that can enlarge the services provided by the professional fields. This development has not been systematized, and the participatory groups have varied in their history.

The encounter movement, a somewhat radical departure, has influenced these developments. There are problems in defining this movement precisely, as indicated in the words of one encounter enthusiast:

> The most frequent criticism from a society that believes in form and structure is that growth centers and practitioners in encounter have never defined themselves: "Are you an educational association, a therapeutic organization, a recreation center, a social club, or a business? Who will be responsible for you? Who will regulate you? What are your ethical standards?" The answers, if I were to formulate them myself, go something like this: "We are all these things

and more. We are seeking a form of human relationship in which man regulates himself, in which few external controls are required because man is fulfilled within himself. We are evolving a new form of leadership in which no one will bear the full burden of being responsible for others. No one speaks for us. We are educating and leading each other. We are not an institution. We are a way of life." This is my personal vision of the encounter experience.[16]

Some of these groups are more identified with the concept of "self-help," but again there is a radical, often belligerent, quality in their attitude toward established organizations. Leonard D. Borman, who organized the first national conference of self-help groups, describes the experience:

Whether we were all relatives or strangers, I sensed a growing awareness at the workshop that the vitality of indigenous activities, expressed through self-help and mutual aid groups, emerged from universal human tendencies. But often in contemporary "official" community life, these were overlooked, ignored, or denigrated. Indigenous networks and sources of support were often enfeebled by conventional institutional techniques of social problem-solving.[17]

Two self-help groups have formed around specific family problems facing group members in common: Parents Without Partners, a support group for the divorced and widowed who are raising children, and Parents Anonymous, a group attempting to deal with their tendency to be violent toward their children.

There are also participatory groups that have a clear relationship with "the establishment." A number of churches have mobilized families into small groups, using a model described as "family enrichment" or "marriage enrichment" which is oriented to enlarging the lives of those who do not view themselves as having serious family problems. Herbert Otto has traced the development of the enrichment movement. He sees it as an outgrowth of sensitivity training, the human potentialities movement, and progress in the fields of human sexuality, family life education, and family sociology.[18] The movement tends to be both religious and secular; the leading secular organization is the Association of Couples for Marriage Enrichment (ACME). The marriage enrichment movement is more mobilized than much of the fragmented field of participatory organizations, particularly through the Council of Affiliated Marriage Enrichment Organizations (CAMEO), to which most of the groups belong.

A somewhat separate development is the family cluster movement. This movement, which was started within the Unitarian denomination but which has spread beyond it, focuses on the extended family.[19] Groups of families searching for family relationships that are broader than those available through the nuclear family join in cluster groups which serve as artificial extended families. These groups offer sources of support, recreation, and commonality, in effect offering the means for a compact among families to provide emotional and other forms of support to each other over time. As might be expected, the longevity of these groups varies greatly.

The trend toward conceiving of formalizing and recognizing family-like activity has even extended to alternatives to traditional marriage, and James W. Ramey has predicted such formalization of other sexual relationships as a potential future replacement for the family.[20] Here the participatory mode comes full circle in relation to the family—from support group to competitor.

INFLUENCE ON PUBLIC POLICY

This brief look at the organizations that maintain a central interest in the family suggests enormous fragmentation. It is important to note that these organizations have not achieved a notable capacity for influencing public policy, although there is a blossoming interest in public policy in some of them.

But if the picture is one of fragmentation and diversity, there may be more common cause among these organizations than has been explored. For example, in 1976 Family Service Association of America (FSAA) had agreements for cooperative activity with the AHEA, the CWLA, the AAMFC, and the ACME. There seems to be a growing receptivity to the concept of coalition as narrow professional interests are giving way to recognition of the importance of public policy to these organizations, even when this interest is derived from varying organizational goals. It is very possible that heightened public activity with reference to comprehensive family policy will help to link these organizations.

HUMAN SERVICES

These family-oriented organizations exist within a larger world generally described as "human services." In some instances, the family-oriented groups operate as functional parts of human service systems; in others, they remain fairly aloof. For example, the more organized family-oriented agencies, such as family service and child welfare, often contract with human service systems to deliver programs directed to families and children. However, they may also act independently, as do the less organized interest groups concerned with the family where there is considerable independence from human services.

Because family-oriented organizations are generally voluntary rather than governmental, the matter of contracting as a means of cooperation with government raises questions that have remained unresolved. Brian O'Connell has written convincingly of the tendency of the contract to destroy the private organization's capacity for social action.[21] There is also considerable pragmatic evidence to suggest that private organizations fare rather poorly in making contractual arrangements with government.[22] Family-oriented organizations, like other private resources, have reason to remain autonomous and to maintain independence from governmental programs. Of course, this adds to the fragmentation which so marks the area under discussion.

A set of questions may be raised about the extent to which program elements in the human services attend to family needs. These concern service delivery systems in health, mental health, welfare, recreation and character building, and education.

HEALTH

The health delivery system in the United States has been subject to increasing criticism in recent years.[23] Views about health delivery are confused and delivery systems are underdesigned.[24]

Attention to the family has had increasing currency in aspects of health care. Perhaps the growing attention in health legislation to the relationship between health and the community and the greater efforts toward comprehensive consideration that have accompanied community health interests have contributed to recognition of the family as a variable in etiology.

Health delivery is deeply involved with specific professional identifications that institutionalize certain directions in health care. The physician is usually the supreme authority, and the interests of physicians are important levers determining the direction of health delivery systems.[25] Therefore, recent developments in family medicine may be considered important influences. A response to shortage in the numbers of general practitioners within the medical specialties, family medicine has been described as "a new concept in medicine" which treats "family units as well as individuals" and practices "continuous and primary health care."[26] Both medical social work and nursing have also espoused the concept of health care service to the total family.

However, the family health perspective vies with many others within the field. Interest in disease entities, the development of health care institutions, such as hospitals, and the necessity to limit services to avoid skyrocketing costs have all militated against a complete acceptance of the family health care model. Medical insurance is available for family protection against disease entities, but not for consideration of family dynamics themselves. Health maintenance services may be provided through such prepaid arrangements as Health Maintenance Organizations, but most Americans do not have access to this more preventive, and often family-oriented health service. Linkages between community-based family-oriented, organizations and health facilities are often tenuous and uncertain. One must conclude that family health care in the United States is not yet fully integrated with overall health service delivery methodology, nor is the potential for using the family's protective capacities fully exploited within health regiments.

MENTAL HEALTH

In the development of psychiatric theory, family relationships have had a prominent consideration. The psychoanalytic theoreticians as well as the adherents of later schools of psychiatric throught viewed family relationships as primary etiological agents in individual mental illness and mental health. Many of the ensuing therapeutic procedures, however, tended to ignore family relationsips, and individuals, rather than families, were the focus of treatment.

As mental health services developed, child guidance clinics tended to be the most directly related to the total family, while mental health clinics tended to be more aloof from involvement with family members. Mental hospitals also treated individual patients, though the development of family care homes indicated an appreciation of the family or a family-like setting as a resource in post-hospitalization recovery, but these efforts to consider the family were exceptions. In fact, the individualistic approach was so pervasive that even family service agencies tended to adopt a similar approach, in spite of their theoretical orientation to the family. An interesting comparative study of mental health clinics and family service agencies, using data collected during the 1960s, indicates surprising similarity between the two kinds of organizations. Both family agencies and clinics were seeing disturbances of family and social relationships as their most common presenting problems, and focus on the family did not differentiate the two settings in the kinds of services provided.[27]

With the development of the concept of comprehensive mental health, concern for the family as one element in the community came to the fore. The Joint Commission on Mental Health Care of Children stated in 1970:

> Many needed services do not exist, and many existing ones are lacking in quality, quantity and coordination. Obviously this situation strongly affects families as well as children and youth. Beyond this, services tend to be focused on individuals rather than on the family as a unit. Parents are frequently asked to carry out a host of sometimes conflicting operations related to specific requirements for their individual children. Thus family life itself may become further disorganized by the very services that are meant to help, and their good intentions merely amplify the forces already present in society which tend to undermine the unity of the family. Families are generally asked to adjust to the many diverse requirements set up by educational, health, and social service agencies. Little thought and recognition is given as to how these various service systems can adapt to the requirements of the family as a dynamic whole.[28]

With the spread of comprehensive mental health as a concept, focus on the family became more integrated with some mental health practice. The problem was that it proved difficult to implement the concept nationwide and a faltering economy also led to disturbances in the allocation of governmental funds. Conflicts among both clinicians and politicians meant that the implementation of comprehensive mental health varied greatly. Interpretations of the meaning of comprehensive mental health differed across community lines, and a family orientation was not always a facet of even the newer mental health systems. The Joint Commission's statement is as appropriate in 1977 as it was in 1970. The director of the National Institute of Mental Health, an important federal organization encouraging the development of local community mental health centers, has publicly despaired regarding progress in mental health research, with emphasis upon community concerns, seeing 1967 as a key year.

> By 1967, four years after passage of the Centers Act, the community mental health centers program budget had overtaken the amount of money available for research. Research had not been downgraded as a programmatic priority, nor had research funds been channeled toward the services program. Rather, a leveling of the growth curve that had first been detected in 1964 became more pronounced. The traditional research program and budget, that is, the number of new grants and dollars awarded, became static and other components of the Institute grew around it.[29]

The organization of mental health services has not expanded to meet total family mental health needs, and the immediate outlook is not encouraging. Comprehensive mental health services, a hopeful and interesting design for service integration and breadth, appears now to be stalled as a major development in human services.

WELFARE

The American welfare system seems to have moved toward a subdivision of services—those directed to public assistance, and care programs, particularly for the young and old. Both of these are of interest in considering American service approaches to the family.

Public assistance in the United States has been a source of political controversy for some time. A complex political process surrounded efforts at reform in the Family Assistance Plan; these shall be considered later in this chapter. Probably, Aid to Families with Dependent Children (AFDC) is the most family-oriented of the categorical assistance programs; it also happens to be the most controversial. Eleanor Judah states the situation well:

> AFDC, a program universally castigated, remains our basic legislation to supplement and support poor families with children. In only 26 of the 50 states are families in which both parents are in the home but unemployed included in this program. In 24 states they are not included. Family breakdown is actually made an eligibility condition. A policy, though an unwritten one, permitting high unemployment to curb inflation at a time when exclusion of the unemployed from the basic provision for families is allowed, is an example of the tacit policy of the federal government. Using the criteria to evaluate policy of inclusiveness, adequacy, equity, and ease of administration, the AFDC program is found wanting on all counts as a provision which supports and supplements family well being. While it has been castigated even by Presidents as responsible for family break-up, no substitutes are currently being considered.[30]

This questionable program is directed to ten percent of the families with children in the United States and to twelve percent of the children. More than half of all female-headed families are utilizing AFDC assistance.[31] Nearly one-third of all the children whom AFDC supports, who are not supported by a father, were conceived out of wedlock.[32] These and additional statistics indicate that there are special social and emotional problems for the children in families that AFDC supports. Yet very often the system is not supportive of the available family structure.

Title XX of the Social Security Act passed by the Ninety-Third Congress has become the means by which social services are administered within the federal-state system. Federal provisions allow considerable discretion by states in the development of their services. Among five stated "national goals" to guide the development and delivery of social services, the third goal seems most relevant to this discussion—"preventing or remedying neglect, abuse, or exploitation of children and adults not able to protect their own interests, or preserving, rehabilitating, or reuniting families."[33] Although it is early to evaluate the significance of this legislation, particularly in relation to a complex and disparate set of state responses, there is no apparent great wave of family-oriented programs developing from Title XX. Usually the state programs have maintained responsibility for the direct care of children who would otherwise be abused or neglected. The emphasis has been to substitute governmental services for those of families conceived to be inadequate or nonexistent. The record of this substituting activity appears to be extremely bleak. Paul Mott developed a report for the Subcommittee on Children and Youth of the United States Senate.[34] This examination of government-sponsored care services for children is a serious indictment of the present system. Mott notes that "the largest share of our available resources is allocated to provide foster care rather than supporting the biological family or placing children for adoption."[35] Mott's examination of the data suggests:

1. That the longer a child stays in foster care the less likely he or she is to return to the natural home and the lower the probabilities of adoption.[36]

2. That there is inappropriate turnover among professionals who supervise foster care programs.[37]

3. That for all practical purposes, children in foster care are "lost." Officialdom is unaware of the child and his needs, and it has no goals for his development.[38]

4. That children with special needs are particularly barred from adoption.[39]

5. There is a serious shortage of foster care facilities which results in children being inappropriately placed in institutions.[40]

6. That relationships between organizations concerned with child care are chaotic, and the organizations are incapable of appropriate cooperation.[41]

This study compared the use of foster home services with

potentials for aiding families themselves, and Mott recommends the following legislative goals:

1.   Increase the resources and competence of families to cope with their problems in order to prevent unnecessary separation of children from their families;
2.   Attempt to identify family problems and possible breakup early so that resources can be mobilized to prevent breakup if this is desirable;
3.   Mobilize services to restore broken families as viable units as quickly as possible where appropriate;
4.   If restoration of the family within the time period relevant to the child's need is not possible or appropriate, freeing the child for adoption as quickly as possible and placing him or her in a suitable home; and
5.   Completing and implementing a stable foster care plan if, within a time period relevant to the child's needs, the child cannot or should not be restored to his or her original home or placed for adoption.[42]

In summary, the Mott report indicates that the present system of public foster care services is not properly oriented to the family, that it is inefficient and inappropriate, and that fairly complete reorientation of children's programs is necessary to provide the services they need.

The American welfare system has been less clearly responsible for the care needs of the other major dependent group, the aged. A series of supportive services have emerged, however, that support the care of the aging, ranging from subsidy of institutional arrangements, sometimes through third-party payments, to in-home support services such as homemakers and feeding programs. Financial support has been provided through Supplemental Security Income, as well as through the Old Age and Survivors Insurance system. In these programs, there have been disincentives to marriage for some recipients. Again, the trend has not been particularly directed toward the possibilities for family experience among the aged or support of the family system which might be a care provider. Geraldine M. Spark and Elaine M. Brody have examined research which indicates a potential for the continuance of social relationships and care facilities through extended family ties.[43] It appears that the possibilites for family involvement with the aged remain largely unexplored within the public welfare system.

It is a peculiarity of the American welfare system that nomenclature (Aid to *Families* with Dependent Children, Divison of *Family* Services) and an accompanying value system seem to indicate that family needs are given high priority. The Children's Bureau statement of adoption standards exemplifies this point:

> The family is viewed as the principal socializing agent for the child with the schools, health, recreational, religious, and law enforcement institutions serving a secondary but highly significant role in socialization. Assurance that children and youth are reared under conditions that favor development, use, and realization of their individual capacities is held paramount. The primary purpose of child welfare services is to recognize family dysfunction which impairs the growth and development of the child and provide the habilitative and rehabilitative services either in cooperation with or independent of the family.[44]

There is tension in this statement between expression of respect for the force of the family and a governmental response which substitutes for it or supports it. The evidence suggests that welfare services in the United States tend to attempt to substitute for the family and, in doing so, can be indifferent to the potential of the family itself.

RECREATION AND CHARACTER BUILDING

Organizations such as the Boys Clubs of America, the Boy Scouts and Girl Scouts, 4-H Clubs, Campfire Girls, and the YMCA and YWCA have retained an ancillary interest in the family over the years. This interest has often been expressed in their goal statements and sometimes in program content. Organizations whose membership is made up of young girls have related particularly to skills development for homemakers, and the Y programs have had occasional educational programs geared to family life. The general trend of these programs, however, has been toward the enrichment of individual lives through physical education, recreation, and programs geared toward group activities. Thus, it is significant that the national YMCA has moved directly into concern with the family and has instituted a family enrichment program, the Family Communications Skill Center.[45]

EDUCATION

In Chapter 1, Ogburn's thesis that the family has lost some of its functions in modern times was discussed. One of the functions lost, he suggested, is the educational function, which the schools have taken over in an organized way.[46] The relationship of the school system to the family, whether rival or partner, has remained an unsettled one. Parent-teacher associations have emphasized support of school administrations rather than integration of the family and the school. School social work, often the official link between the school and the family, is a relatively undeveloped field, with most school systems lacking fully developed departments. It is not uncommon for parents to feel ill at ease in schools and with educators; schools are for students, and rarely can the rest of the family find a place in the system.

The rivalry between family and school seems to be persisting. Recently, there has been a mounting campaign to involve schools in extending their services to younger children in order to provide universal day care services.[47] This movement, supported by some teachers' unions, was bitterly attacked by one child advocate in Congressional testimony in 1975; considerable research was cited calling into question the school's competence in providing services to children with special needs and indicating that schools do not have the capacity to provide day care.[48] A set of potential standards for judging the worth of a child care program included a requirement to encourage services and settings that support the family and are relevant to the child's own culture and environment, and that are staffed by people from the child's own community, including parents. It was urged that parents be given the central role in the community's decisions about the types of services to be provided in the day to day operation of the programs in which their children are participating. It would appear that these are early warning signs in what may become an important conflict of ideas in years to come concerning the roles of the family and of the school in child care.

It is in the matter of day care that the issue of family versus school seems to be most accentuated. Arthur Emlen has been a steadfast critic of educational influences in day care.[49] Out of his own favorable experience with a family-oriented day-care approach, he decries the removal of children from parental control and interest. He believes in building upon parental interest rather than substituting for it. With the growth in the number of employed women, there continues to be pressure for more nearly universal day care. The way this problem is resolved may have considerable import for the future of the family as a socialization mechanism in early childhood.

SOCIAL MOVEMENTS

Thus far, organizations that provide direct services to families have been discussed. These structures have some effect on policymaking, but another perspective is needed in order to understand the environment for family policymaking. Certain social movements have developed as arenas for political action and have influenced public policy. They have provided a means for intellectual exchange and debate. At the same time, they have influenced public opinion, broadly speaking, in regard to the relationship of the family to the public interest. Industrialism, organized religion, human rights, feminism, and alternative lifestyles are all social movements offering centers for thought and action which influence the perceptions of policymakers regarding the family.

INDUSTRIALISM AND THE INDUSTRIAL CORPORATION

The effects of industrialization must pervade any consideration of family policy in the United States, and it is necessary to return repeatedly to differing perspectives on the subject. Here the large industrial corporation as a social movement affecting family policy and program is examined.

The corporation is inherently oriented to its own survival.[50] It is not surprising, then, that most corporations are primarily concerned with how the family serves—or fails to serve—the corporation, if, in fact, any concern for the family is expressed at all. Corporations have shown a long-standing interest in the spouses of executive level personnel, sometimes formally but more often informally. The underlying question behind this interest is whether the executive's spouse and family will provide support for the executive's functioning within the corporation.[51] It is well-known that family and marital disruption can adversely affect worker productivity. Leo Perlis speaks for both labor and management in saying:

> Management wants productivity and production and, therefore, a stable labor force, high morale, low turnover, and a minimum of absenteeism. The union wants better working and living conditions for its members and their families—a 'happy' fellowship of productive working people and concerned citizens.[52]

A series of service provisions ranging from counseling to child care services, from company welfare funds to extensive family health plans, from consumer schemes to legal services, have been developed in large corporations. They have been recommended by either labor or management or both and have tended to be responsive to the nature of the work force required. For example, employment of large numbers of female personnel might lead to an industry's providing in-plant day care. These kinds of services are not provided out of an altruistic motivation but are viewed as necessary components of a productive enterprise.

But industries *have* shown their altruism through participation in the United Way movement, corporate foundations, or other activities which have had an effect on services to families. (There are also incentives for such activities related to public relations and taxes.) Some corporate or industrial managers have demonstrated a sophisticated self-interest, recognizing that community tranquility is related to a stable work force and an uninterrupted consumption process. Hence corporate contributions to social programs have been justified as aiding the business environment. In any case, in most industries expenditures in services to the family either inside or outside the corporation are a small portion of return on investment. Nor do United States expenditures directed to helping the family deal with the work environment compare in magnitude with the fairly extensive investment by European nations.[53]

Given the predominance of large corporate industry in American life, and its tendency to see the family as a resource to be manipulated, either as worker or consumer, it is doubtful that industry will make any sacrifices in order to strengthen family life. In fact, the differences between the corporate and the familial lifestyles and the potentials for conflict between the roles of worker and family member would suggest a deep antagonism. The corporation's interest lies in a placid family, one oriented to work and expressing malleable consumption values. Where family needs are irrelevant to corporate interests, indifference or even suppression is likely to be the corporation's response. The emphasis of industry must be on keeping things as they are; ultimately, industry must be a force speaking against the development of a national family policy if it is directed to substantial change in social and political patterns.

ORGANIZED RELIGION

For purposes of this book organized religion may be treated as a social movement. Although it is possible to argue that there are indications of the church's losing influence, it remains an extremely important force in American life and has a deep and complex role to play with reference to the family and, ultimately, family policy. Both marriage and the family are celebrated by nearly all religions, and there is an almost universally acknowledged relationship between the family and religious belief.[54] All major churches treat marriage as sacramental and provide support within their structures for traditional family experience. Beyond its doctrinal role, the church is often a medium for the expression of ethnic solidarity. The boundaries around an ethnic system are most permeable through intercultural or interfaith marriages, so that the church as a social grouping may reinforce strong feelings about who are eligible mates and the status of the family within the ethnic group.

Churches have been active in a number of ways in programs supportive of family life. For example, there are specific Jewish, Roman Catholic, Lutheran, and Episcopalian auspices for family-oriented service programs, on the pattern of American voluntary charitable organizations. The clergy has moved into the area of pastoral counseling, with many clergymen trained in marriage and family counseling.

From the foregoing, it would appear that organized religion

would be a naturally strong advocate for families in the policy arena. In fact, however, the church at large has not been a force demanding public policy development for the family. Despite the growing ecumenical spirit in American religious circles, the differing views of the family and the maintenance of ethnic boundaries through the church have proven effective barriers to coalition in respect to policy. A decade ago, one policy-oriented public figure, Daniel P. Moynihan, expressed the view that organized religion is a major force blocking the development of family policy.[55] He has also observed that coalitional efforts have been unsuccessful because of deep underlying differences between denominations.[56]

What are some of the causes for this ineffectiveness? The following are suggested reasons why American organized religion is unable to function with unity in family policy:

1. **Pluralism.** In the United States, organized religion provides an arena for the support of nearly all political positions. Certain denominations are known to espouse conservative or reactionary social values while others are proud of their social liberalism.

2. **Doctrine.** In most denominations there are theological definitions relating to marriage and family. These definitions differ markedly from one denomination to another. The meaning of sexual differentiation in social roles, marriage and divorce, birth control, and the relationship of individual conscience to church dogma, all are readily recognizable areas of doctrinal difference which form a base for major differences in the conclusions reached in regard to social policy questions.

3. **Ethnic boundaries.** Because the church is often a reflection of its ethnic constituency, it carries a usually informal role in boundary maintenance and its actions must have some relevance to its constituency. For this reason, it may be difficult for churches to move in the direction of broad, overarching policy areas and maintain a strong advocacy role.

4. **Secularism.** The familiar American problem of conflict between church and state may be acute in the area of the family. It may be imagined that a stronger public role in regard to

family policy will be perceived as an intrusion upon the ancient dominance of church authority in the area of marriage and family.

HUMAN RIGHTS

The civil rights movement brought social injustice to center stage in American politics in the 1960s. As this movement evolved, it developed broader interests and has more recently been referred to as the human rights movement. Generally, it emphasizes the position of minorities, particularly those ethnic groupings living in some degree of deprivation. Human rights advocates have worked for an active governmental role in a great variety of social programs. Thus it might appear that family policy would be an important agenda item for human rights advocates. But, although the human rights movement has advocated social programming and ameliorative social policies, there has been difficulty placing this activity in a family context. Probably, the problem dates back to the publication of "A Family Policy for the Nation," often referred to as the "Moynihan Report."[57] Originally a memo to a United States president from an advisor, the report was made public and almost immediately drew a great deal of fire from the black community.

Although Mr. Moynihan had utilized references by black scholars, the report was seen as a white scholar's denigration of the black family. Scalding attacks were made both on the report and on Mr. Moynihan's motives.[58] The central issue was Moynihan's conclusion that "At the heart of the deterioration of the fabric of Negro society is the deterioration of the Negro family. It is the fundamental source of the weakness of the Negro community at the present time."[59] This emphasis on weakness spawned a retaliatory literature relating to family strengths among blacks. In fact, the National Urban League commissioned a major study to consider the strengths of black families.[60] When the emphasis upon strength and special ethnic qualities is on family strength, it is difficult to look at pathology; when the emphasis is on ethnic difference, it is difficult to coalesce with other groups around common problems facing families at large. Thus, while the human rights movement can be seen as a force favoring social programming, the family is not an explicit focus of attention to the extent that it might be assumed.

FEMINISM

Feminism has given evidence of deep concern about the state of the family and marriage. However, there has been an abiding polarity in feminist thought between a position of social revisionism and one of rejection. On the one hand, there have been the writers such as Betty Friedan who advocate wider opportunities for women within a fairly conservative view of family and society.[61] In contrast, a series of writers have emphasized marriage and the family as unnecessary constraints and the means for subjugating women.[62]

This polarity in thinking has prevented coalition among women's liberation organizations in taking a position on the family. The orientation toward protest in the women's movement leads to criticism of traditional family forms, but proposed solutions to family problems are apt to cover a wide range of alternatives. Often, the women's liberation movement strives for social supports to the individual woman in her roles of parent, wife, and worker, as well as for supportive behavior from her spouse. But the prevailing value is that of individual freedom, and support for familial values is at most secondary.

ALTERNATIVE LIFESTYLES

Alternative lifestyles may be considered a product of disturbance in modern family life, but another perspective is also possible. Perhaps because of the immediacy of modern electronic news media, spokesmen for alternatives to traditional family life have effectively enunciated to the public that these options present a system of thought that may be considered a social movement. Experimental living patterns increasingly are undertaken without the secrecy of the past and in open challenge to traditional living patterns. Utopian experiment has been part of the fabric of American life since its inception. However, there has been an increase recently in the number of people choosing alternatives to traditional marriage and family patterns.[63]

This relatively recent development is marked by an experimental quality rather than by a doctrinaire position claiming a superior way of life.[64] In a conference in British Columbia in 1975, the Vanier Institute on the Family attempted to gain experience with members of experimental familial groups in order to develop clearer understanding and definition within the area of alternative familial styles. An excerpt from their draft report stated:

> Many participants described their life situation not in terms of arrival or achievement, but in terms of a beginning or a new experiment. Whether this took the form of involvement in a new familial sociation or a new living context, or both, or even the development of a new way of looking at the world and defining oneself within it, this phase was marked by confidence in life and by a certain degree of enthusiasm. Nevertheless, this confidence did not mask the anxieties and the questioning brought about by the realities of the new life. In every participant's account we always found a relativist view of their respective living situations, accompanied by a constant demythification of 'absolutes,' 'models,' and 'forms.'[65]

It is apparent that these are attitudes that tend to discourage activity in a public policy arena. The necessity to think normatively in social terms is incompatible with an individualistic, experimental approach. Moreover, the impact upon social values that these experimenters effect is unclear. Chapter 2 discussed the social indicators of growing tolerance for alternative family styles. At the same time there has been some evidence of latent conservatism about the family.

THE LACK OF FAMILY-ORIENTED LEGISLATION

This chapter has pointed out that family-oriented groups are fragmented and slow to move, that the human services have not been mobilized to focus attention on the family, and that social movements demonstrate ambivalence and vacillation in approaching the subject of the American family. This chaotic situation surely is affecting the policymaking process. Although family-oriented legislation has been somewhat rare in the United

States, there are two recent examples of federal bills of considerable importance to family life. Their failure to be passed exemplifies the controversy and organizational fragmentation which can surround policymaking even obliquely concerned with the family. Although neither bill was directed to comprehensive policy, both dealt with important components of family policy.

The better-known piece of legislation was the Family Assistance Plan, a response to a fairly universal discontent with the American welfare system. It offered a guaranteed income approach to the problem of family poverty and provided an income floor below which no family would be permitted to fall. Moynihan, as a participant-historian, wrote a remarkable account of the development of this bill.[66] The legislation was well-grounded in experimental demonstration, and the original bill had the backing of carefully accumulated data and evaluation. It was drafted in response to an understood social problem, following a period which had particularly dramatized the plight of the poor in the United States. Moynihan traced the response of interest groups to the legislation and its modifications and found an inability to coalesce, groups unable to direct themselves to established goals, and a trend toward idealistic sloganeering rather than realistic negotiations. He concluded that "the limits of social policy are determined not only by the creativity and boldness of those in office, but also, and earlier, by the capacity of the publics to comprehend and to respond. This limit came quickly where Family Assistance was concerned, as the Congress was to show."[67] Matters pertaining to the economy, civil rights and, most of all, work incentives, came to be central to the controversy surrounding this bill. The original data base and purpose for the legislation became distorted or ignored in the political interchange that finally defeated it.

The second piece of legislation, the Child and Family Services Act of 1975, was considerably less fully developed than the Family Assistance Plan, although earlier versions of it had appeared in the United States Senate.[68] Originally a response to the priorities of the 1970 White House Conference on Children, it had been developed as a child care bill with emphasis on congregate day care.[69] The most recent version of the bill included the concept of developing policy-oriented councils on family life at several levels of government. There were legitimate problems for family-oriented organizations in supporting the bill: the issue of congregate day care as a massive enterprise, costs, and lack of clarity about the purpose of family councils. But the bill was stopped in its tracks by a letter-writing campaign financed by political and religious conservatives who distorted the nature of the bill, frightening many into believing that parental rights would be destroyed by a government that wished to control the raising of children.[70] A subsequent campaign by many socially responsible organizations was incapable of reviving the legislation's political chances.[71] Resources concerned with the family do not easily mobilize as interest groups in the public policy arena!

This demonstrable lack of cohesion helps to explain the paucity of public policy directed to the family in the United States. Etzioni states:

> Organizations or states without a cohesive base have at best a deficient ability to build consensus. They can serve as coercive or utilitarian organizations but not as effective tools of societal and political action, which require a strong normative element.[72]

A national family policy must develop from a value base which has not yet been fully conceptualized. The current efforts to define national family policy may be perceived as the mere beginning of an articulation of social values concerning the family.

chapter 4

A SURVEY OF FAMILY POLICY PROPOSALS

In the late 1960s, some dissatisfaction began to be expressed about public policy directed toward the family. In 1967, Catherine S. Chilman, representing the U.S. Department of Health, Education, and Welfare, offered a description of such federal policies at a conference of the International Scientific Commission on the Family.[1] She emphasized the pluralism in both family forms and government policies, together with the varied family-related program auspices within government. Although the subject was policy, she spoke regarding a multitude of programs. The inference was clear that a coherent, central policy regarding families would be questionable within the American system.

In 1970, Daniel P. Moynihan was raising basic questions about a programmatic approach to policy.[2] He stated, "Increasingly, the idea of system-wide policies commends itself to persons of responsibility in public affairs as an approach both desirable and necessary. We can expect it to be one of the formative ideas of the 1970s."[3] His thesis was that a program approach to problems had been a primary mode of government intervention, and that this approach unduly narrowed perceptions of reality. In contrast, a policy approach could attempt "to encompass the largest possible range of phenomena and concerns. This has its dangers, its difficulties. But I shall argue that increasingly there is no respectable alternative. Knowing what we do about the nature of society and of social interventions, we have no option but to seek to deal in terms of the entire society, and all the consequences of intervention."[4] Using a systems approach, he discussed the complexity of social phenomena, and argued that social policy must therefore be developed in the most comprehensive way possible.

It is the author's contention that comprehensive policy toward the family does not now exist in either federal or state government in the United States. The author is not alone in such a contention, and there is an increasing literature directed toward the subject, perhaps as a vanguard for political activity in the future. But, among Western industrialized nations, it is peculiarly true of the United States that the family is avoided as an explicit object of public policymaking. This chapter will touch upon family policy in other countries and then return to a consideration of policy development concerning the family in the United States, as expressed both in academia and in political activity.

FAMILY POLICY IN EUROPEAN NATIONS

European experiences in particular are assumed to be most relevant to American considerations, because of the developed state of European industrialization, generally comparable to the United States in relative world terms, because of the common cultural heritage of the United States and Europe, and because the continent contains a variety of governmental forms, ethnic heritages, and states of economic well-being. In short, one searches for both similarity and contrast.

Among the European community of nations, the term "family policy" is readily used, although often it is left undefined and emphasizes programs more than policy. Programs directed to families are compared across national boundaries both in the literature and within international organizations.[5] Basic premises in Europe differ from those in the United States. Alfred J. Kahn and Sheila B. Kamerman have probably delineated this fact the most clearly in their book *Not For the Poor Alone*, which examines social programs in five northern European nations through the eyes of American experts in social welfare.[6] An aspect of their central thesis follows:

Our cultural and political traditions say—or are believed by some people to say—that governmental activity in this sphere is probably counterproductive: government interferes, creates delinquency, distorts preferences, perhaps inhibits freedom. We Americans are willing to let government act in specific ways for those already 'deviant,' 'dependent,' or 'failures.' Under these latter circumstances, programs are meant to use controls and serve as instruments of desirable change. To create programs for other people, for people not in trouble, is to insure dependence.

In some European countries people respond to social developments on another premise. At least they seem to want government to do more for individuals in some categories and for families—and apparently have fewer cultural and ideological inhibitions. Some of them say that communal 'solidarity' requires some programs, that individuals have a right to expect services, just as a government has a right to expect responsible citizenship and tax payment. The result seems to be less-inhibited social innovation or experimentation in program forms in the social services. Since programs are designed for the typical citizen, for any citizen, not just for the dependent and the cast-offs, programs can be of good quality and need not be demeaning. Limitations that arise stem from limited knowledge and skill, bureaucratic and organizational problems, and resource constraints—not from a cultural fear that social services good enough for anyone will be over-utilized and will subvert deeply held values.[7]

This approach is carried into family-oriented programs. In September 1973, a conference of European ministers responsible for Family Affairs meeting in France, affirmed the principle "that it is not enough to concentrate action on the families which are obviously in a poor situation but also on other families which apparently have no problems. They considered that it is important to make the social services more accessible and so attractive that families of all categories would feel it natural to use them."[8]

Moreover, a basic policy orientation is built into government concern with the family through the constitutions of many European nations. For example, the Federal Constitution of the Swiss Confederation requires that the Confederation "shall have due regard for the needs of the family," and thereafter gives specific powers and limitations to the means by which government may carry out this duty.[9]

The United Nations held a European seminar in 1961 on changing family needs, for which G. Desmottes wrote an interesting review of family policy in Europe.[10] His analysis concludes that comprehensive, explicit family policy is a product of the twentieth century, required as a defense against the incursions on family function brought about by industrialization. He views the "sociological rediscovery of the family" as the mainspring of policy interest, which was followed by an interest in child care and development, dealing with "family deficiencies," improving the quality of housing, and supporting the economic value of household work.

Desmottes comments upon the identifiable administrations within governments with responsibility for family policy and cites specific family departments in France, Belgium, Luxembourg, the Federal Republic of Germany, the Netherlands, and Portugal. He points out that in some nations family policy may be subsumed within "ministries of social affairs."[11] He also describes what he considers family policy orientations in European nations and discusses:

1.   The public sphere's extension of services to the private sphere (the family) with due regard for retaining privacy and intimacy.

2.   Family allowance and social security legislation.

3.   Support for the family as an institution.

There is considerable attention given to avoiding dependence upon the state, and having family members retain personal initiative. But Desmottes raises some question about nations' successes in achieving this goal.

By 1974, the costs of social programs were becoming prohibitive in Western Europe, and efforts to cut back were developing. Moreover, new efforts at being selective about who would receive the benefits of social *programs* were beginning to challenge the preceding universalistic philosophies. Conversely, comprehensive social policies, pursued with a long-term perspective, were gaining favor.[12]

It is difficult to identify family policy in individual nations. Kahn and Kamerman state:

For some, family policy and social (or societal) policy are

synonymous. Others define social policy as the umbrella concept, while family policy is one sub-category, along with labor policy, population policy, etc. Some view family policy as an autonomous domain, similar to such others as health, education, housing. As such, family policy would include family law, services to families and children, family oriented income transfers, and so forth.[13] In some instances, the family may be considered an instrument for other policies. Hence, "family policy" may refer to a perspective on the family as a means to carry out educational, service, or social control policies. Or, it may be considered a perspective or criterion for policy development and, therefore, is interrelated with all other policies.

In view of the differences and complexities involved, it is impossible to discuss family policy developments in Europe comprehensively. It is clear, however, that from whatever perspective and however defined, it has been pursued more actively in some western European nations than in the United States, illustrating that government may be actively and explicitly concerned with the quality of family life and may provide policies and programs related to families without intending to weaken the family as an adversary institution.

The Union of Soviet Socialist Republics and those nations within her orbit in eastern Europe present a somewhat different picture. In the U.S.S.R., there has been a considerable change in policy toward the family, including a full reversal of the policy toward marriage and divorce that was in force during the first few decades following the revolution. The current view of the family is that it is an instrument for providing training and collectivization, and, thus, a means to an end. Under the circumstances, there has been no hesitation in attempting to regulate and direct the family's existence and functions.

Friedrich Engels originally described the family as a means by which one sex was subjugated to another; he proposed that the care and education of children should become a public matter and that the new state should work for the dissolution of the family.[14] The divorce process was eased, but experience with the social realities of crime and delinquency, the cost of child care, and popular support for the family led to a reorientation between 1934 and 1936. Since then, the family has been recognized as important for child rearing and emotional satisfaction. However, it continues to be considered a means for collectivization, subordinated to such other collectivities as the school and the factory.[15] When it is believed that the family is failing to instill the "socialist morality" in its children, the state may remove them. The family may be considered on trial, being under evaluation by more important collectivities. The explicit precept in the U.S.S.R. is that "the peer collective rivals and early surpasses the family as the principal agency of socialization."[16]

This use of the family as a subordinate instrument of governmental intent is repugnant to the Western democracies whose efforts tend to be directed toward the support of the family as an end in itself. The Communist case illustrates that family policy may not be entirely benevolent toward the family, however comprehensively conceived.

WHY THE LAG IN THE UNITED STATES?

The Western democracies continue to find comprehensiveness elusive in developing their family policies. In the United States, where the intent to develop family policy is not yet firmly established, incoherence reigns. John Romanyshyn characterizes the situation as follows:

> We have extolled family life but have rarely nurtured it in this society. We have sought to strengthen family life without providing the basic institutional supports essential to enable the family to perform its basic functions. We have in short, very little in the way of a national family policy. Instead we focus on individual and social problems. So powerful is our emphasis on the individual that, for the most part, our programs designed to deal with social problems have tended to ignore the fact that the individual is part of the family unit.[17]

He goes on to cite surveys of laws and regulations that indicate the lack of references to the family in American governmental activities directed to social concerns.[18] Why is it that the United States, so often a leader in social developments, so connected with world affairs, so often viewed as the epitome of the industrialized society, is backward in developing government policies in support of the family, even as the very characteristics of American society require such action?

There are profound reasons for the government's posture in this respect, among which are the structure of government and attitudes toward the family relating to individualism, privacy, and pluralism in lifestyle.

As already mentioned, the United States Constitution is silent on the subject of the family. In order to understand this omission one must consider the circumstances in which the Constitution was originally written, along with the trend in contemporary societies to turn from an emphasis on status to an emphasis on contract.[19] The needs of an emerging industrialized society called for the capacity to avoid inherited status and to bring workers into an expanding economy as fully as possible on the basis of their abilites. The system of inherited social status, so much a part of the English monarchy of the time, was to be avoided in the new American society. The possibility that the family might occupy central attention within the American Constitution posed the problem of the maintenance of a nobility. The implicit contract of the Constitution was to be between government and the individual citizen, without reference to the family.

A vacuum was thus created, because the federal government was to avoid direct consideration of the family. There needed to be at least a regulatory function to define marriage, divorce, inheritance rights, and so forth. To fill the gap, the body of law generally referred to as family law became a matter for individual states to develop and administer. From the outset, therefore, government actions toward the family could not be coherent; a barrier to comprehensive national policy was built into the institutions of government. The pattern continued as social welfare services were developed by the states, providing a patchwork quilt of services addressing family problems, often obliquely.

Perhaps the value most central to a concern for the family is the individualism that has become institutionalized in the American system. It is a long-standing assumption that the rights of the individual outweigh those of the family and that too much attention to the family may interfere with individualism. Nearly a century ago, Sir Henry Maine characterized the movement toward modernism as the "gradual dissolution of family dependency and the growth of individual obligation in its place. The individual is steadily substituted for the family as the unit of which civil laws take account."[20]

Possibly related to this individualistic bent in the United States is the view that home and family are bastions of privacy. The borrowed phrase, "an Englishman's home is his castle," has come to mean that the family household is the final barrier to governmental intrusion. So long as family and state are seen as counterforces, the question of how the state may be of service to the family does not arise. The notion that government action must be intrusive has been reinforced by the fact that social programs have been directed to specific family problems rather than to the population of families. Shirley Zimmerman has stated:

> In other words loss of freedom and independence, intrusion into family affairs are perceived as proper exchange for society's largesse. These perceived terms of exchange have been artfully used to arouse and perpetuate fears regarding the development of social policy for the family. Insofar as government is concerned, then, the family is strictly off limits, except under well defined and accepted conditions.[21]

The assumption that governmental activity is inherently regulatory poses additional problems for the development of family policy. To address the family in a comprehensive policy sense is somehow to grapple with the ethnic and cultural pluralism so characteristic of American life. Familial behavior may be expressed in a plethora of lifestyles. Alvin L. Schorr has stated the situation from the viewpoint of practical politics, as follows:

> Our origins are plural and, in contrast to other western countries, relatively recent. Although families of various national, cultural, and ethnic backgrounds have at times appeared to be converging toward common patterns, negotiation and compromise among diverse interest groups are our political mode. The absence of agreement on family goals would appear with greater clarity if it were not masked by a tendency to broad moralizing. Thus, all groups hold the family to be of primary importance if one goes by statements of principle. It is in the political marketplace

that it becomes clear how diverse are the definitions of family and how different the goals for it. The tendency has in fact been to avoid making such choices, regulating very little and failing to enforce what has been regulated.[22]

SOME PARTIAL PERSPECTIVES ON FAMILY POLICY

Recent years have witnessed increased thinking about governmental posture in relation to the family. Janet Giele has expressed her expectation of a breakthrough in family policy in the United States in the next decade.[23] The term "breakthrough" does seem appropriate here, because a major shift is required to move beyond our patterned responses to national family policy. Appearance in the literature of material related to the development of family policy in the United States is not entirely new, but its volume has increased markedly in the current decade. An early writer on the subject was Alva Myrdal who, like many of the early writers, tended to equate national family policy with a specific prescription for governmental behavior.[24] For Myrdal, this was a population policy. Later writers, particularly in the 1960s, tended to take primary interest in family income schemes.[25] A review of the literature suggests that there is an increasing sense of comprehensiveness in defining national family policy, but there continue to be more narrowly conceived views which reflect certain perspectives. Some examples follow.

Income policy. Equating income policy with family policy has become somewhat more sophisticated, but the trend continues. It is often seen in writing about the position of the black family in society, notably by advocates for blacks. Robert Staples has written a detailed set of proposals for public policy that would be supportive of black families.[26] At the center of this program is a design for a guaranteed income coupled with greater activity against discrimination in employment. In addition, he proposes a subsidy for family-oriented services such as child care centers, child placement services, and free contraceptive services and abortion.

Andrew Billingsley, writing from the black perspective, also stresses economic security and access to employment, but he takes a fairly extreme position concerning the responsiblity of society to insure that the family functions:

> If the family in all of its variety is viewed as a subsystem of the larger society, then the enhancement of the functioning of family life is the responsibility of the larger society more than of the individual members of the family.[27]

In Billingsley's view, the family is a recipient of what society has to offer, and its pathology is a reflection of societal inadequacy. He believes that government should take an extremely strong role in correcting its own shortcomings.

It is not only the minority perspective that leads to a perception of family policy as primarily concerned with income. John M. Romanyshyn utilizes social class theory in combination with views of family life stages to justify his emphasis on income policies and social mobility through enhanced work opportunities in an "ideal model" of family policy.[28]

The feminist perspective. The feminist perspective has also provided a springboard for discussion of policy. Jessie Bernard, describing dissatisfaction with culturally determined sexual roles, suggests that family policy might provide a corrective.[29] She recommends attempting to eradicate poverty as a baseline but emphasizes policies that minimize the social and economic costs of reproduction to women. She is not explicit about the policies she advocates, but it is clear that she is concerned with role formation and the internal relationships between husbands and wives in marriage, where she sees women as victims.

A somewhat less subjective feminist position is expressed by Joan Aldous, who focuses on the growth of two-career families and sees family policy as a means of accommodating this new family form.[30] Like Bernard, she recommends more flexible and shorter work hours to accommodate child care, looks for child care centers to aid in the process, but goes on to advocate that both sexes receive training in homemaking skills, and that further research be provided to better understand the issues facing the two-career family.

The welfare service perspective. There is also what may be described as the welfare service perspective in family policy. This is somewhat less well developed in the literature, perhaps because the approach evolves more from fields of practice than from scholarly works, and its connection with national family policy is not always clearly defined. The emphasis is so programmatic that it can seem removed from interest in the policymaking process, but its effects are extremely important. An article on family policy by Jacquelyne A. Gallop illustrates this perspective. She mentions the need for an adequate income for every family, an open educational policy, and the availability of health care, but her emphasis is primarily on a minimum income program and what she feels is the weakness of the nuclear family. She concludes:

> Family policy directed toward supporting the family's role in human development must chart a course which results in provision of services directed toward enhancement of social confidence. These will need to include services directed toward restoration, maintenance, and enhancement of family and individual social functioning. Such services in themselves will not necessarily differ from current ones but their availability and accessibility will. It is imperative that our commitment and approach to service provisions change. Social services must be seen as a right and as a necessary ingredient to self-actualization. Services must be based upon recognition of the interdependence of individuals, families, and institutions in today's social order. Societal acceptance of this interdependence would be measured by institutional change and decreased residual social welfare approaches to social problems. Then, and only then, can we move toward social welfare as a goal of society.[31]

Gallop's notion that social services will eventually become less necessary if they are expanded does not disguise her clear perception that, under current circumstances, family policy is the enlargement of social welfare and social services.

The regulatory perspective. It is also possible to approach family policy from a regulatory perspective. It has been noted that the concept that government must be regulatory is a pervasive one in American life. Often this perspective is expressed in efforts to revise family law—divorce laws, support arrangements, child abuse statutes, and the like. Amitai Etzioni has enunciated the regulatory position as he has raised questions about the ease of divorce.[32] In his views, social controls are dangerously out of favor, exaggerated searches for happiness prove quixotic and injurious to family life, and the need to return to a sense of duty calls for government encouragement.

ATTEMPTS TO DEVELOP A
COMPREHENSIVE APPROACH

Efforts at comprehensive family policy prescription are very recent. Marvin B. Sussman was one of the authors of early efforts in 1971.[33] He moves from a systems approach to a suggestion that family policy be more thoroughly researched and urges the establishment of a national research and advocacy center on the family. He also feels that the pluralism of family lifestyles requires client-centered service approaches and research to develop such methods. Income guarantees and education for family life are the foundations of his approach to policy.

Schorr, whose views were mentioned earlier, has long given consideration to family policy and has repeatedly espoused children's allowances. He feels that government activity to redistribute wealth will be necessary for an adequate family policy. He also recommends the development of firmer social indicators concerning the family and family impact analysis and a fairly complete reconsideration of the purposes and methods of the social services. Further, he believes that social regulation in regard to the family must be extended.[34] In his writing he tends to describe family policy in nonincremental, even radical, terms. This is coupled with his recognition that governmental response is vastly different from his prescriptions and he is pessimistic about the possibilities for the development of family policy.

Urie Bronfenbrenner has been a persistent and influential commentator on the relationship of the state to the family.[35] In his work he has tended to concentrate on the functions of the family in raising children and the interface between the community and the family.[36] He presented a proposed "American Family Act of 1974" to the Senate Subcommittee on Children and Youth, which outlines very specific recommendations for Congressional action.[37] The proposed Act is fairly comprehensive, humane, and a reflection of current wisdom about the state of the family. His recommendations are worth outlining here:

1. A program context which is "family centered rather than merely child centered."
2. Support of part-time work possibilites.
3. Programs geared to deal with the major forces of social

debilitation: poverty, loss of family members, two parents working, parents working on different shifts, and neighborhood breakdown.

4. "Involvement of other adults and other children in the care of the young."

5. A comprehensive approach to "health, education, and social services."

6. Child care options.

To these ends, Bronfenbrenner suggests "revision of welfare and work legislation," and he gives a partial list of measures to achieve the objective:

1. Welfare reform to favor part-time work as a means of providing child care, including state payment of the poor to care for children at home part-time.

2. "Legal prohibition against unlimited compulsory overtime for parents with young children."

3. Antidiscriminatory personnel policy provisions for part-time employees who are parents of young children.

4. Incentives for business and industries for family-oriented activities, for neighborhood and community activites which benefit families, and for activities in schools to involve "other children" in the community.

5. Assessment of the impact on the family of the use of homemaker services.

6. Group day care.

7. Enhanced training for child care workers.

8. Community commissions to develop recommendations concerning the needs of families and children.

9. Outcome evaluation for programs directed to families.

10. "A family-centered employment policy in the federal government."

Bronfenbrenner's approach goes a long way toward the development of cohesive and comprehensive family policy. One may also question the possible effects of his proposals on traditional child care practice within the family, his lack of focus on the quality of marital experience, and the involvement of the aged in the family. Moreover, is his emphasis on group day care consistent with his comments about providing options to families?

Nonetheless, he has provided an important model for the development of family policy which can be expanded and embellished.

Probably the most ambitious endeavor to explicate an American family policy is Mary Jo Bane's book *Here to Stay*.[38] Bane is unusual in her optimism about the progress of the family as an institution, but she seems some tension between the family and society at large:

> Family privacy, family responsibility for children, sexual equality, and equality of opportunity are principles to which American society is strongly committed, at least in its rhetoric. Many of the issues facing the society today involve conflicts between these principles. In this sense, the problems cannot be 'solved.' Instead specific situations must be explored; and principles reconciled when possible, weighed when not.[39]

For her, the most serious question is the issue of child care, and she supports means by which parents can have both careers and family life. Yet universal child care schemes are too expensive, as are extensive child care leaves from employment. She suggests an increase in child care programs and also a concentration on equalizing the division of home and child care responsibilities between husbands and wives through new provisions in both family and personnel law. There should be family law reform directed toward increasing the rights of children, while recognizing the concurrent problem of reducing the rights of parents. She favors social insurance rather than social welfare designs in specific programs directed toward families, and she looks for such designs to provide greater incentive for a commitment to the family.

THE METAPOLICY ORIENTATION

All of these attempts to produce a comprehensive family policy are disappointing. The reason may lie in part in the nature of public policymaking. Yehezkel Dror has written a full description of the process of making public policy.[40] The first stage, metapolicy making, is characterized by the need to "make policy about making policies."[41] It is clear that national family policy is still in the metapolicymaking stage. The writers cited above may have been attempting to use the perspective of later phases of policymaking, which do not accord with the current political reality.

Fortunately, some of the literature on family policy is beginning to take on a metapolicy making coloration, with a greater sense of both the systematic sequence necessary to produce public policy and the recognition of the present state of political activity and potential. For example, Zimmerman reasons that policy development requires knowledge of the family as well as understanding of social policy.[42] She analyzes the conflict between the values of individualism and those of the family which has forestalled policy involvement. However, her review of social indicators about the family establishes the implication that further effort in the policy arena is required, particularly policies to "insure the viability of the family as a social system throughout its entire life span," even at the cost of losses to individualism and unrestricted freedom.

Sheila B. Kamerman and Alfred I. Kahn have also produced an unusually perceptive article.[43] They raise a great many unanswered questions about the consequences of the government's fragmented programmatic approach and make a case for cohesive and explicit policy directed to the family on a systematic basis. They include in their definition of family policy: specific programs and policies to achieve explicit goals; programs and policies that impact upon the family without agreed-upon goals; and governmental actions and policies not specifically addressed to the family, but affecting it.

They elaborate further upon the differences between "explicit family policies" and "implicit family policies," purposes which are "manifest" or "latent," and consequences which are either "intended," "unintended," "direct," or "indirect." From all this they infer that family policy is "both a field of activity and a perspective." They make an important distinction when they indicate "it is probably essential in the analysis of family policy to differentiate the interests of the family as a unit from those of particular roles and statuses within the family."[44] This is a pivotal choice which disagrees with some other writers who equate family policy and social policy.[45]

Kamerman and Kahn categorize the fields of activity for family policy as population policy, family planning, "cash and in-kind" transfer payments, employment, housing, nutrition, health policies, personal social services, child development, and social policy for women. However, they point out that there are consequences to the family in policies concerning taxes, the military, transportation, land use, and the environment. They recognize both liberal and conservative biases against family policy but return again to the fact that government cannot but affect family experience and that it is a myth to assume that laissez-faire is possible in the modern age. Recognizing that the "arena for action is broad," they urge: the development of a "family impact statement" as a routine element of policy developments; the systematic study of the interplay of formal social services and child care programs, and informal social networks; and comprehensive study of American family policy. Although they see a risk if family policy develops as a restrictive and regulatory instrument, they also see it as one foundation for effective social policy.

There is a compatibility between the writings of Zimmerman, Kamerman, and Kahn which makes them considerably different from the diverse and fragmented suggestions about policy directions comprising the materials discussed earlier. It is clear that they are written from a metapolicy orientation.

RECENT EVIDENCE OF MOVEMENT

So far the literature cited has been heavily influenced by an academic perspective. To what extent is there evidence that the development of comprehensive family policy is a "real-world" concern?

Norman V. Lourie, in his presidential address to the National Conference on Social Welfare in 1976, heralded the birth of a new age:

> One very exciting development with promising policy implications for the future, has been the growing interest by Congress, academia, public and voluntary service organizations, and the general public in the trends and pressures affecting American families.

Senator Walter F. Mondale, whom we're honoring this week, stimulated this interest by convening subcommittee hearings in the Fall of 1973 entitled 'American Families: Trends and Pressures.'

Current recognition of the importance of families, and to a large extent, traditional families, comes as no surprise to this gathering. Our educations and experiences reinforce our convictions.

The essential importance of families has been largely forgotten or overlooked in recent decades. In some respects, and in some circles, it became unfashionable to talk about the importance of families.

I don't know why this change has occurred, but I do know there is now again a widely held belief that the family, however constituted, is the most important institution in this country. It is families, now and throughout history, that have had the unique ability to instill ethical, moral, and cultural beliefs in their children, and to shape human thought and emotion.[46]

One may surmise that Lourie is right. There are several straws in the wind—in bureaucratic behavior, in increased coalition among family-serving organizations, and, most telling of all, in political behavior. By the end of 1976, several important developments had occurred.

The 1970 White House Conference on Children and Youth set high priority on the development of a major child care bill, with particular emphasis on day care.[47] Over the ensuing years of legislative drafting, as mentioned in Chapter 3 in a somewhat different context, a bill was developed and gradually enlarged to concern itself with family policy, or at least the machinery for its development. By 1975, the then-named Child and Family Services Act included the development of "child and family service councils" on federal, state, and regional levels which would "approve goals, policies, action and procedures of prime sponsors, including planning, personnel, budgeting, funding of projects, and monitoring and evaluation."[48] Although the bill never came close to passage, it was significant in increasing the salience of family policy with a number of interest groups.

Individual states sometimes took notice of the federal activity. California developed its own bill along similar lines.[49] Other states were beginning to consider statewide approaches to family policy and one, Florida, mounted a fairly ambitious state policy development program.[50] A large, statewide conference was held, followed by the development of a Task Force on Marriage and the Family Unit. Among its recommendations to the legislature were: programs for premarital information and counseling, family life education in public schools, the establishment of a family court, new definitions within family law, aid to families caring for children or aged who might be institutionalized; welfare reform, and a policy of continuing public review in both executive and legislative branches to insure that family needs were met.

There have also been increasing signs that interest in the family can be used politically. Early in the 1976 presidential campaign, Sargent Shriver, then a candidate for the presidency, developed a fairly complete statement on policy concerning the American family.[51] This part of his ill-fated campaign attracted a surprising amount of support and enthusiasm.[52] Subsequently, the successful candidate, Jimmy Carter, developed his own statement on the family. His vice-presidential choice, Walter F. Mondale, had been the chairman of the Senate Subcommittee on Children and Youth which had developed the Child and Family Services Act. Mondale had been a primary promoter of the notion of a family impact statement and was apparently influential in bringing this element into the campaign.

As a presidential candidate, Mr. Carter employed a coordinator on the family, Joseph A. Califano (now Secretary of the Department of Health, Education, and Welfare), who researched issues of family policy and developed a "Report to Jimmy Carter" which proved to be influential in subsequent campaign speeches.[53] Citing social indicators and program data from the federal government, as well as economic data, Califano emphasized particularly the problems besetting American families. To solve these problems he recommended: increasing opportunities for employment; placing consideration for the family as a basic premise of federal policies and programs; and increasing understanding of the ways in which public policies affect American families. Mr. Carter later called for a White House Conference on the Family as a means to develop broad participation in family policy development.[54]

Another development has been the joining of governmental and academic interests as family impact analysis has developed into a small movement. In 1973, Margaret Mead appeared before the Senate Subcommittee on Children and Youth, which was having hearings on the general state of the family. She made an impassioned presentation, focusing on the need for government to be a central force in the development of policy and more particularly the need for analysis of how governmental programs affect the well-being of families.[55] Senator Mondale later began to consider this idea as a basis for legislation.[56] At least in its formative stages this approach has had a useful but negative quality. For example, Mondale said in October 1974:

> We are talking, for the first time, about setting up a system that would require a family impact statement to force Government to discuss and debate the possible consequences of a given policy on the family. It would be similar to the environmental impact statement.

In the same interview, he also stated:

> All public policy should be designed, at the least, not to interfere with the family's job of raising stable, self respecting, ethical, moral Americans.[57]

Born from the legislative process, there has been considerable detailed work on the family impact analysis approach. The Foundation for Child Development has financed programs related to the subject at George Washington, Columbia, and Vanderbilt Universities.[58]

As a foundation for this movement, Sheila B. Kamerman developed a document that is basically a feasibility statement.[59] She defines a family impact statement in the broadest possible terms, describing multidisciplinary knowledge development, development of social indicators, and development of family policy as subsets for the development of a statement. A question for the future remains. A family impact statement has usually been defined as a means to check both existing and proposed legislation to insure that it is not harmful to family life. It is possible that such a definition could actually lead to a lessening of legislative involvement with the family because of the difficulty of developing legislation which would "pass" such a statement. The easiest way to do no harm may be to do nothing!

To this date the bureaucratic, not the legislative, side of government has produced the most comprehensive statement of family policy. In 1971, the National Research Council of the National Academy of Sciences received a grant from the U.S. Department of Health, Education, and Welfare, Office of Child Development, which commissioned an Advisory Committee on Child Development charged with four tasks:

1.   To review the combination of unmet needs of and the unrealized opportunities for child development up to age eight.
2.   To develop the goals and essential features of an integrated national policy for child development.
3.   To assess the implications of scientific knowledge for public policy.
4.   To make recommendations for new program initiatives both within OCD and in other federal agencies having responsibility for the development of children.[60]

To carry out this charge, a five-year study was launched. In late 1976, the findings were reported in *Toward A National Policy for Children and Families.*[61]

The Advisory Committee interpreted its charge to relate to the state of the American family and produced policy findings and recommendations that have a comprehensive quality, although they emphasize the care of children and thus only one major family function. The recommendations favor income redistribution and economic supports to allow parents to give full-time care to children under the age of six. In addition to recommendations on health, day care, and services for children with special problems, there is also a strong plea for greater investment in research: "(a) studies of children and families in natural settings; (b) systematic experimentation with, and evaluation of, proposed programs for children and families; and (c) the development of social indicators on children."[62]

The report is a thorough effort at policy analysis and development. The strength of the report, an intensive consideration of early childhood care in America and potential policy responses, is also its weakness; the report is limited to establishing linkages between early child care and other aspects of family life. The discussion of potential community-based programs to serve family child care functions is too narrowly based to allow for a comprehensive social service approach. Nevertheless, because of its depth, this report promises to be a reference work in family policy development for years to come. With accompanying political support, one might foresee bureaucratic initiatives for a move toward greater orientation to the family.

Though substantive suggestions for family policy differ considerably, and include subtle shadings of variation, some common areas of concern are obvious. There is also a suggestion that powerful interests are apparently converging on policy-related matters. However, the outcome is much more difficult to predict. If family policy making requires a major reordering of social priorities, what will have to be done to develop the needed support? What definitions of the family can be used to build coalitions rather than divisiveness? How can the family be an attractive subject for practical politicians? There is also reason to question the appearance of a wedding between political and academic forces. Are politicians really defining their activity in family policy as are the academics? One wonders whether a politician, speaking of "the family," has in mind the diverse familial living arrangements, pluralistic values systems, and ethnic backgrounds that are in fact the pieces of the mosaic of family life in the United States. One may wonder also whether politicians who need to demonstrate as dramatically as possible that they are advancing the nation can give heed to the importance of preparatory information and theory development. One can expect that energy will be consumed in this area in the near future, but whether heat or light will be produced is as yet undetermined.

chapter 5

RECOMMENDED COMPONENTS OF A NATIONAL FAMILY POLICY

The preceding chapters have repeatedly restated the author's underlying thesis: that a cohesive, comprehensive family policy has not yet evolved in the United States and that it is crucial to the welfare of both families and the society-at-large that private interests and government begin the long and difficult process of formulating such a national policy. Whatever American family policy now exists is the sum total of the various policies and programs that, however inconsistent and incoherent, make an impact upon the family. The development of a policy blanket, as it were, for the family poses issues of both costs and risk. Consequently, coherent family policy development must compete realistically with the alternatives of doing nothing or retaining the problem-oriented, programmatic point of view of current policies. In other words, the need for a comprehensive policy must be compelling. Because ample documentation of the reality of the need has already been presented, it will only be summarized briefly here as a prelude to discussion of both the values that the author believes to be essential foundation stones for the construction of family policy and what the components of such a policy should be.

A growing minority of Americans experience family breakdown, an experience that differs markedly from many of their values and expectations, and that often occurs without adequate cultural supports to help them through it. In the process, many children are raised in disturbed conditions and learn attitudes toward family living that will affect the next generation of families. One may raise questions about what this means to the public good. If many Americans are deeply unhappy and besieged by problems, is this not a public concern? If children's basic learning experiences about their relationship to society often occur within troubled families, is this not a target for intervention? And, in a nation that prides itself upon equality of opportunity, if many families can be shown to be particularly disadvantaged is this a burden the nation can carry indefinitely?

The available data also reveal a phenomenal growth in what has become a commonplace American lifestyle—the female-headed family with children—a style that is found most frequently among the poor and the disadvantaged minorities. If it is the American purpose to challenge the cycle of poverty, this family lifestyle must be given social supports.

Moreover, there is evidence that greatly expanded opportunities for individual choice in lifestyle and in interpersonal behavior are affecting the family's performance of its functions. There is some indication that the rapidity of these social changes is causing at least temporary family disturbance leading to a lessened ability to perform the functions society requires for its survival.

Having established that there are valid reasons for developing national family policy, the author has also outlined some of the formidable obstacles to be faced: a lack of public awareness, the fragmentation of family-centered organizations, gaps in knowledge of family trends, preoccupation with programs rather than policy analysis, and the assumption that the governments activity will be regulatory in nature. Any serious proposal is likely to be met by a counter-proposal. Advocates and adversaries will inevitably draw up battle lines!

A POTENTIAL "CRITICAL MASS"

But even in the face of such formidable obstacles as these, one can dimly see the shape of a potential "critical mass" likely to develop within the next few years—events occurring that will influence a change from inaction to action. Three components of this critical mass are as follows:

1. **Organizational interests in family policy.** Organizational interest in mobilizing influence directed toward national family policy would appear to be an important precondition to policy development. There is considerable evidence of new interest by family-oriented organizations in matters of public policy. In fact, the speed with which organizational activities related to family policy development are being adapted is virtually explosive. At the end of 1976, the following eight national organizations either had implemented, or were planning to implement, activities related to national family policy within the years 1976 or 1977: American Orthopsychiatric Association, Association of Couples for Marriage Enrichment, Child Study Association—Wel-Met, Council of Affiliated Marriage Enrichment Organizations, Family Service Association of America, Groves Conference, The National Academy of Sciences, and the National Council of Family Relations. Many other organizations were attending conferences sponsored by these groups, were participating in academic activities related to family impact analysis, or were implementing projects funded by foundations interested in areas related to family policy.

It remains to be seen what this interest will produce. Commonly accepted definitions of national family policy have not developed, despite the interest. Efforts at coalition are as yet imcomplete. National family policy development will require great tenacity, and serious students of the matter with whom the author has spoken worry about the sudden popularity of the idea. It may have been too quickly accepted and, difficulties once faced, may be equally easy to abandon.

2. **Centralization and institution development.** One important barrier to public policy development previously discussed has been the lack of a location within government for consideration of the family. Some specific, ongoing bureaucratic interest in the family as a central concern would appear to be a necessary prerequisite for policy development. One step in this direction is a proposed White House Conference on the Family, called for in the 1976 presidential campaign. The potential for making the family cause visible and retaining official government interest in such a

conference, seems high.* It must be recognized, however, that a large, nationally based conference would also expose the current fragmentation and extent of discord about national family policy.

One might hope also for some centralization in the process of working out contractual relationships between government and the voluntary sector. A series of difficult questions evolved from experience with government contracts to date, and there is evidence of governmental behavior injurious to private organizations.[1] If such contracts become a keystone of the governmental approach to program development directed to families, the contracting process will require attention and remediation. Perhaps most important of all, a "family bureau" within the government might provide a new locus for assembling knowledge concerning the family and the services the family requires. Legislators and interest groups could look for both leadership and data from such an operation. Ultimately, linkages could be made between governmental departments by means of the family bureau's assigned function at the interface of departmental programs concerning the family.

The mandated value orientation of such a bureau would be critical in forming enough support for its establishment. Even a hint that such a bureau intended to mold American lifestyles could quickly undercut its formation or continuance. The mission of a family bureau would have to be the preservation of a specifically American value system. And it will be necessary to legitimize a comprehensive approach to social policy. If comprehensive policy is to be developed within a family bureau, comprehensive approaches must regain the acceptance they lost in the disillusionment of the 1960s.

3. **A constituency for the family.** Because volunteer activity with reference to social causes is peculiarly characteristic of American social behavior, it is particularly ironic that effective citizen interest in the condition of the family, or organized lay activity devoted to it, is relatively insignificant.[2] Volunteer interests have become professionalized and volunteers relegated to small

---

*At this writing, the Department of Health, Education, and Welfare is active in preliminary planning for such a conference, but a specific program has not yet been developed.

groups such as boards of directors or, in some instances, as volunteer workers in secondary service roles.

Only recently has lay interest in the family taken a new form, the participatory group. These groups have usually formed as self-serving, commonweal groups, but the possibilites are intriguing that they will develop a mass interest in the family. It seems questionable that such groups can retain membership interest without giving some consideration to the social environment.

One may wonder whether the United States is on the verge of developing a family constituency such as has developed in many European nations where, as has been mentioned, family unions with clear political interests abound. If so, the particular combination of sociability, self-actualization, and social action that such groups might offer could well begin to establish a constituency for the family beyond the social welfare bureaucracies that are often dismissed by decision makers as interested only in program perpetuation.

Another direction for the development of a constituency concerning the family seems promising. A variety of institutions with educational components, from schools and churches to clubs and social agencies, has taken part in such activities as parent effectiveness training, transactional analysis, family life education, family development programs, or family enrichment exercises. Educational sophistication is developing about family life, and with it some awareness of the family's fragility, the complexity of choices contained within familial behavior, and perhaps some recognition of the fact that the social environment affects it.

There does seem to be some evidence of a critical mass for support for new governmental initiatives. There are, however, obstacles, indicating that the formation of family policy may require an incremental approach. A governmental response to the family is unlikely to be revolutionary in form; consequently, gradualism is the mode of policy development that will occur.

METAPOLICYMAKING

Earlier, the author began to utilize Yehezkel Dror's concept of metapolicy.[3] The concept is particularly helpful in approaching such an underdeveloped area as national family policy. Metapolicymaking provides a safeguard against the trend toward isolated problem solving by defining a set of ground rules for policy development. According to Dror, metapolicymaking concerns establishing general guidelines for making policy, and it is in the spirit of Dror's definition (rather than in an exact use of his outline) that the author attempts to organize his own metapolicy recommendations. Much of what Dror describes as metapolicy-making is to be found in earlier chapters or is implied in what was described as preconditions. In this sense, this entire work can be considered as metapolicy development, directed toward finding a way to take hold of the policymaking task ahead.

The recommendations and conclusions that comprise the balance of this chapter are based on the assumption of continuing change and cultural diversity and on a view of the family as a resilient and *necessary* component of a society striving for individual and social betterment. The question, then, is how the larger social system can protect and enrich families, not harass and disorient them. The following metapolicy considerations are proposed to advance this goal.

Each recommendation is introduced by a basic value statement derived from what has been learned so far. Then, certain problems, defined as a clash between these values and the reality of family life, are addressed. The allocation or reallocation of resources is considered, and alternatives in opposition to the recommended actions are discussed.

FAMILY FUNCTIONS

Family policies should emphasize support of, rather than substitution for, family function. Family members have functional relationships with each other and increasingly seem to exercise choices in the manner in which they define and utilize these relationships. The family group itself must be functional. When it is not, its own cohesion is threatened and interpersonal processes within it are distorted.

Moreover, these functions of the family are vulnerable to competing organizational patterns which may substitute for them rather than support them. This is particularly true of socialization and enculturation. The family may be weakened rather than strengthened by overly active methods of "help."

Implicit in current American policies are several undesirable alternatives:

1. **Encouraging other groups to carry out family functions.** This approach is convenient to certain professional interests, because it transfers areas of legitimate activity from the family to other organizations. But the likely outcome of continuing such a policy direction will be to weaken the family further by discouraging it from carrying out its functions.

2. **Considering individuals instead of families.** For example, "children's rights" are sometimes advanced without reference to family and parental systems. The emphasis on individual pathology rather than on the social system in mental health is also illustrative. Although this emphasis can sometimes usefully simplify a helping process, it may also distort reality by systematically ignoring aspects of etiology.

3. **Considering the family as a component of other social interests.** Family functions may be considered within larger contexts. For example, education within the family is only one aspect of all education, or family consumption may be considered one aspect of the total economy. The subject of family probably cannot be totally isolated, the family interacting as it does with its social environment. But inattention to the family and its own mechanisms does little to protect the family and the social utility contained in those interactive processes.

In the following pages, an active governmental role with regard to help for families will be discussed. This governmental role must be to help families carry out their functions when there is considerable personal or environmental discontinuity.

In a world in which both parents are apt to be employed, separations and divorces are frequent occurrences, women are often called upon to maintain the family, and institutionalized substitute-care services tend to be inadequate. The family must play a role in determining the very nature of the service arrangements designed to serve it. Supporting services should not overwhelm the family; rather, they should encourage the family to retain the practical and viable parts of its function. Some ways to do this are discussed below.

Families, both nuclear and extended, are the backbone of care for dependents in the United States—the young, the old, and the handicapped. When the family is unable to perform its care functions, one tends to think of institutional care or other substitute care, but family policy supportive of family function might direct itself more to helping the intact family or kin network become more capable of giving care. A variety of incentives might be provided, both through the tax structure and through direct subsidy, to encourage the family to retain its care-giving functions. The extended family might be a resource which as yet has not been examined. For example, extended family members are usually excluded as paid foster parents when substitute child care arrangements must be made. "Family care" for adults rarely utilizes extended family members but instead pays unrelated families to open their homes to strangers. Bureaucratic control rather than family control of the arrangement is emphasized.

Of course, there are many situations which do not allow for either nuclear or extended family care arrangements. When family members are unavailable, there is clearly a need for substitute arrangements outside the home. A comprehensive family policy *must* have a strong day care component because the need is crucial and is worsening as more mothers go to work outside the home. Family day care is one incompletely explored possibility. Because it is a familial procedure rather than an institutional arrangement, children are enabled to have more family experience—particularly important in view of the predominance of corporate, nonfamilial experiences children experience in an industrialized society. It need not be simply an inexpensive alternative to "quality" day care that uses formal methods of early childhood education; with proper design and administration it might well provide a quality of care that can compete with other types of programs.

But another factor is worth further exploration. Urie Bronfenbrenner's concern with the disappearing community as it affects children was discussed earlier. Many parents prefer neighborhood arrangements to institutional day care, and the nation needs to find ways to support the efforts of parents to provide day care for their children with people they know and with whom they can retain a degree of parental control. The family day care visualized here, then, would include aid and subsidy, when necessary, for parents to contract with other parents for the care of their children, with the arrangements being monitored and enriched by professional facilities. Day care should not be a process of giving children over to any resource, but rather a participatory design that includes encouraging the parent to be a continuing party to the arrangement. This concept of day care may be extended to other types of need such as care for the retarded child who cannot be kept at home and, possibly, even care for an isolated elderly family member.

It is possible that the very young child represents a special case requiring a different kind of care. The recent report of the National Academy of Sciences states as a basic principle:

> No child under the age of six should be deprived of the needed care of one (or the only) willing parent simply because that parent has no choice but to work outside the home to enable the family to exist at a decent standard of living.[4]

Despite the fact that an extensive review of research results bearing on this statement was made by the advisory committee that prepared it, and no conclusive evidence was found that children are harmed by early substitute care when the quality of that care is satisfactory, there is reason to believe that stability in early family experience is extremely important as one of several variables influencing personality development. The prevailing view seems to be that sensitivity to stress is inversely related to age, and the age of six is commonly used to describe the upper limit of these more sensitive years.[5] This view would suggest that a useful component of national policy would be the provision of incentives to keep a parent at home with the very young child. What is proposed is an incentive to remain at home, not a requirement to do so.

SATISFACTION IN THE MARITAL RELATIONSHIP

Marriage should be satisfying, and, when it is not, termination of the marriage is an appropriate alternative. Individual satisfaction within the family, and particularly within the marriage, has become a keystone in family experience and Americans are increasingly willing to reconstitute their families when their expectations for satisfaction are not met. Policy has followed practice, as state laws reflect a liberalization of the grounds for divorce. In turn, marriage increasingly has become a serial matter as adults choose new marital partners when old ones do not satisfy.

Direct regulatory measures to stem the divorce tide appear to be the wrong focus. The view here is that the weight of evidence suggests that social evolution is in quite the opposite direction: Americans demand satisfactions from their families, notably in the marital relationship, and insist on opting out of marriages when there is too little satisfaction. It follows that public policy will be required to be responsive to certain living conditions that must be accepted as part of the outlook for the family: marital partners and families who search for satisfaction and personal growth within their relationships, an element of choice in the continuation of a particular family grouping, and the sequelae of divorce and separation—interludes of single-parent family structures and reconstituted families. If families search for their unique brand of satisfaction, the means to help them to do so would appear important. It would suggest that counseling facilities and enriching group activities should be available to all American families. (Both the auspices and the consideration that this should be a combined public and private arrangement will be discussed later.)

Continued attention must also be paid to the problems of the high-risk family form, the single-parent family. There must be services to ameliorate the particular disadvantages that this family experiences in society. On somewhat similar ground is the need to consider the reconstituted family. Although this family form is often successful, very little is known about the obviously complex cross-familial relationship, the parenting styles involved, and the outcomes for child development. There is a basic job to be done in providing specifically tailored counseling and group opportunities for families of this sort.

Besides direct services, there is the matter of transition between one family state and another. Usually, this calls for regulatory law, which develops primarily at the state level. Variations among state laws have led individuals to try to match law to the occasion by going from state to state, with other parties to matters connected with family transitions unable to utilize the law fully as residents of different states. In other words, there is a major problem of coherent justice in an area of increasing legal activity—separation, divorce, support, and so on. It would appear that a more consistent set of laws covering these areas is required in the *national* interest. Should this be accomplished through federalization of aspects of family law, or through strong federal recommendations for the standardization of state law? It also appears that the trend toward liberalization of family law should continue.

LIFESTYLE ALTERNATIVES

Family policy should support individuals in making satisfying choices of familial lifestyles which are compatible with the requirements and commitments necessary for the maintenance of the society. Family members are faced with a variety of lifestyle models, and they have increasing freedom to fashion ways of living that uniquely meet their individual needs. Lifestyles that only a few years ago carried social taboos are now possible, so that the range of options has increased dramatically, to the bewilderment of many. The issue now is whether to delimit the alternatives as dangers to the social fabric and family life. Should there be further regulation and should greater structure be imposed? Historically, American society has tended to enlarge, not limit, options available to individuals, and it appears unlikely that greater limitations could be usefully imposed. Furthermore, a governmental effort to mold personal living patterns would be incompatible with American conceptions of freedom.

A technology for birth control and the growing emphasis on eroticism in society have also affected lifestyle choices. Perhaps as one result (no doubt affected by other variables), marriages are occurring later, often preceded by periods of sexual activity. As the means for controlling fertility are now available, patterns may be chosen that do not include the expectation of having children. Sex without marriage on the part of heterosexuals, as well as sex on the part of homosexuals, is likely to continue to increase. It is appropriate, too, that the trend toward acceptance of varieties of sexual attachment between consenting adults will continue to be reflected in law.

Furthermore, significant aid to family life may be associated with the situation. Delayed marriage after a period that may involve exploring other options could encourage a capacity for a more considered approach by an individual contemplating marriage and family. There is no question that the desired family is more successful than any forced familial arrangement. It is ironic that premarital sexual experimentation is often cited as an indication of family downfall when, in fact, it may very well be a means to support the heavy load placed upon family experience in a modern era.

Once again, as one approaches family law as connected with these optional lifestyles, there appears to be reason for work toward a permissive and comprehensive national law.

PLURALISM

Pluralism should be a guiding principle in framing family policy. Families reveal a bewildering array of structures. Much of the sociological writing of this century has centered on the highly mobile nuclear family, disconnected from its geographic roots, responsive to the call of industrial opportunity, and separated from a kin network. Such a prototype family may exist, but there is growing recognition that many families do not meet this description. Many ethnic groups retain strong kinship ties, sometimes supported by geographic proximity in ethnically oriented neighborhoods but also at great distances with the aid of transportation and communication capabilites. If neighborhoods are disappearing, as some suggest, it does not necessarily follow that the extended family is also disappearing.

The style of these kin networks—not all of them blood relationships—varies considerably between individual families and between ethnic groups. Sometimes these relationships are symbolized by honorary titles such as "uncle" or "aunt." Frequently they are important aspects of family life in low-income neighborhoods where family-like arrangements may be particularly functional for reasons of protection, income, increased social opportunities, and so forth.

Pluralism in family lifestyle is indeed a widely accepted aspect of life in the United States, with its wealth of ethnic diversity. As discussed here it transcends what is usually described as alternative lifestyle and tends to be traditional rather than radical. A poorly conceived family policy might evolve that did not take this into account. Particularly if the family becomes popularly accepted as a target for policymaking, there is the danger of total, rigid identification with the most obvious of family groups—the traditional nuclear family. Artificial extended families, old-world family patterns, or other manifestations of diversity could be looked upon as alien to family interests and discouraged, as they often were when the melting-pot myth was in vogue in the United States. The danger, of course, would be that manifestations of productive familial behavior could be weakened through too great a structural emphasis. Family policy must not be discriminatory; it should encompass many subcultures within American society.

What is surely needed is a redefinition of the family so that it can be viewed as a functional unit rather than simply a series of genetic connections or eternal, unvarying relationships. It must be recognized that functional definitions are exceedingly difficult to draft. Without functional definitions, however, government is likely to respond inappropriately to matters of family experience. Function indicates social utility; it can therefore be the means for defining the family and supporting that which is socially useful.

Any new definitions of the family that are drafted should reflect the reality of pluralism, and also be consistent across state lines. Matters of family definition cannot safely be left to variable state law in an age when ease and frequency of travel make it possible to manipulate such a system. But consistency in law should not require uniformity in family performance. Functional definitions should allow for the variety of structures of lifestyle upon which Americans can be expected to insist. Structure and function are not the same; similar functions may be carried out with all the variety that the mind of man can create in personal relationships. A family must be defined as that which functions as a family, not a preordained set of relationships.

Where service programs directed to families are supported by government, a pluralistic response seems called for as well, particularly in areas directed toward interpersonal relationships. The lively interest of private organizations in the family, and the growing use of the contract as a means of carrying out governmental interests through the service capabilites of the private sector has been discussed. Yet this has been occurring at the same time that governmental services have tended to dwarf the resources of the private sector. This would suggest that there is considerable room for growth of contractual arrangements between governmental and private resources, and a service strategy might well be developed around the principle of utilizing pluralistic service capabilites through the use of such contracts. In turn, voluntary groups could be encouraged to reflect ethnic and cultural variety and develop specialized services. The effect might well be a more diverse set of services providing much greater access to families because of their suitability and understandability for groupings of families. Emotional and social isolation from services, now a frequent problem in the United States, might be greatly ameliorated.

In order to utilize fully the potential of the contract to mobilize private sector resources, important and far-reaching changes would be required in human service planning activities and in the premises on which they rest. For the private human service organization there is the problem of maintaining autonomy and independence—which one leader in the field of mental health says cannot be done.[6] Moreover, it is eventually likely to lose its own options as its resources become tied to government-approved programs. In the short term, this might be acceptable to the government as contractor, but there are serious long-term problems in such an approach. Ultimately, the private agency would become quasi-governmental in that its program content would be determined by government. It would be faced with the harsh option of accepting this condition or withdrawing from the government contracts market. In either case, the possibilites for pluralistic program development, which the contracting process is well-suited to encourage, might be lost.

But it is possible for government to follow another design. The contracting process could provide considerable support to the institutional needs of the service provider.[7] Private sector service providers for the family could well be regarded as national resources, worthy of being maintained independently. For example, adequate compensation could be provided and unduly arduous accountability procedures could be avoided. Government contracts could be a source of strength if they supported an agency's program and if they included compensation for administration and independent program development. Clearly, accountability for goal attainment and performance standards is necessary, particularly if pluralistic patterns of service provision are encouraged. Difficult trade-offs between the inefficiencies of service duplication and the value of consumer options would be required. But the gains in enlisting the pluralistic private sector would appear to outweigh the risks and costs.

KNOWLEDGE BUILDING

Family policy must be based upon knowledge. To reiterate, the literature about the family is massive, but its quality leaves something to be desired and the knowledge base upon which it rests is seriously lacking. Not only is the literature repetitive, but basic research is in short supply. Often the scholarly literature has obscured the basic importance of the family as well as the need to understand better such an important institution.

A knowledge base about the family is more controversial than might appear. In the past, tradition, ethics, and even sacraments have provided guideposts for policies concerning families, but it is precisely because traditional values are now being challenged that traditional responses are inadequate and a body of accurate and complete knowledge is required. Because our understanding of the family is so tentative and incomplete it will be important to avoid overdependence on any particular data set or sector of knowledge. Instead, it is necessary to maintain a comprehensive and evaluative intelligence function.

As has been seen, social indicators concerning the family tend to emphasize what is happening to family structure. The work done by the U.S. Bureau of the Census is extremely valuable to policy development, but the lack of a corresponding effort to understand why structural changes occur and the attitudes behind change is a serious gap in information. Family function must be a central concept in policy development, and the meaning of structural change cannot be understood without comparable analysis of change in function and attitude.

There is another serious knowledge gap concerning the idea of exchange between the family and society. Definitions of exchange are bewildering in their variety. Nevertheless, both the range of this literature and common experience would suggest that the function of exchange is quite real, even if an understanding of it is inadequate. More sophisticated information about this function is necessary in order to defend the cost of governmental concern for the family and also point the direction for intervention.

Furthermore, in order to develop an adequate family policy it is necessary to know a great deal more about a number of phenomena discussed in this book. What, for example, is the value or utility of various lifestyle options either to individuals or to society? Which options should be supported? The author's metapolicy recommendation for relative freedom of choice might be changed if evidence becomes available that some lifestyles are inherently more functional than others. Do reconstituted families require services and programs specifically tailored to their needs? It is known that single-parent families face a number of environmental disadvantages, but there is little basic information concerning the actual functioning of this family form when environmental disadvantages are controlled.

The questions raised above are suggestive only of the many questions to be answered through research. Some of them call for continuous sampling approaches as well as sophisticated rating methodologies and survey techniques. Surely they suggest the need for resources which can underwrite large-scale research under governmental sponsorship and greater national centrality in the collection of data and the financing of diverse research activities. Without such research our knowledge base will remain a shaky foundation for the development of public policy.

INDUSTRY

Ways should be found for industry to better support family life. The family both supports and is supported by the work place, not only through economic exchanges but also through more subtle sociological and psychological processes. Family members often are directly affected by what happens at the breadwinner's work place and the total family is clearly lined to the organization that supplies its income. Yet there is an imbalance in attention given to the family as compared to the work place. There is a degree of compatibility between the long-range interests of industry and those of the family which may be utilized in the development of many areas of family policy. Incentives for corporate enterprise more fully to consider family matters would appear helpful in harnessing these common interests.

It has been observed that geographic mobility puts particular strains on both the nuclear family and its relationship with its kin. This is a source of family strain which can carry spillover effects, such as costs for child care or related family disturbance. Government itself, as the largest employer in the nation, could set an important example in considering more carefully the transfer of workers.

It has often been the case that geographic transfer has been offered as the means toward upward mobility within far-flung work settings, public or private. If new policies were instituted in regard to transfer of workers, care would be required to avoid a loss of option by the worker through entrapment and immobility in matters of job advancement. If the matter seems complex, it is certainly no less so than other areas of personnel activity and no less available for modification by personnel practice.

Because national family policy would be required to support economic well-being, it would lean in the direction of "full employment," whether that term meant public employment or macroeconomic measures to increase jobs. Given current social trends, one could expect this policy to continue to draw increasing numbers of women into the employment market. The need for increased day care has been discussed, with particular stress on a family day-care model which utilizes neighborhoods and activity by parents. This emphasis is not meant to exclude other possibilites for day care. One major innovation, modeled on European experiences, can be more fully developed—day care furnished by industry itself. Aggregate day care using an early childhood education model seems particularly applicable to the work place.

Child care is not the only service the work place might offer the employee's family. Many large employers form mutual support groups, often through union activities, which provide opportunities for recreation, joint purchase, loans, and so forth. A few even provide employee counseling services.[8] Public policy enlarging industry's consciousness of the family might include the provision of tax incentives for companies to develop such services.

The greatest impact of all might be made simply by expanding options in regard to the hours of work. Mothers could plan their work time in conjunction with the hours their children are away from home, particularly in school. Moreover, the parents could share more equally child care and work responsibilities if they could mesh their schedules, with each caring for the children while the other is working. Also personnel policies that would support family life through such provisions as the mutual timing of vacations, adequate time for the marital couple to be together through shortened work hours, or time off to care for sick children could greatly decrease family disruption and discord. Obviously, there are constraints upon the capacity of industry to offer flexibility in work hours, but the illustrations suggest some important possibilities for aiding the cohesion of family life. For example, the government might offer tax incentives for arranging flexible working hours. Much could also be done within industry itself, perhaps through pay differentials to recover the costs for the privilege of flexibility or part-time employment.

Housing is an industrial product that deeply affects family behavior.[9] Yet housing regulations have developed primarily around such issues as safety, physical quality, and financing procedures. Little attention has been paid to housing as a physical environment for families, at least in a regulatory sense. The varying requirements of a family for housing at different life stages and greater understanding of the impact of housing upon families should take their place among the many regulatory considerations in housing and land use. One can see the possibility of an organization within the Department of Housing and Urban Development which is focused on the development of practical ways to consider the family and its needs within the American housing market structure.

INCOME

An income standard of decency should be promulgated in the United States for all families. This value has provided this entire study. The matter of income is related to employment, as discussed earlier, but considerably more needs to be developed in this area. A seeming inconsistency has been expressed in this chapter: the need for children, particularly for those under the age of six, to have greater opportunity for continuous care from parents and the support of the option of employment for all adults. It is in this area that the conflict of values that most insistently plagues the family policymaker must be faced. Children need care from their parents, but parents also need freedom to make choices about employment.

A trade-off now must be considered—the social value of employment against the value of child care. For some time, feminists have disagreed with the process of American economic accounting because of the omission of family household work as an aspect of national product.[10] There is a need to determine the cost involved when housework is lost in exchange for paid employment. More appropriate income tax devices could then be developed based on the worth of housekeeping. The choice to go to work should be available, but some cost sharing should be involved, particularly where governmental subsidy of child-care arrangements is necessary. The less measurable social cost of loss of family process might also be a consideration as cost sharing is explored.

In regard to maintaining a minimum level of income to insure decent family life, a case may well be made for major income redistribution. But such an approach seems fairly radical to Americans and conflicts with other widely held values. It is therefore doubtful that a major redistributive program will develop in the United States in the near future.

There is generalized concern, however, with the present system of public assistance. Public assistance programs have lacked public support, the Aid to Families with Dependent Children

(AFDC) program in particular. Study of this program, including the social conditions within which recipient families exist, has produced the most dismal of findings.[11] There can be little doubt that the family on welfare functions on a less than adequate income and is exposed to a series of other social disadvantages that receive little effective attention. A national family policy must do better.

The problems with establishing a minimum income program that satisfactorily meets family needs are great. These are such formidable political, economic, and social barriers that there is general agreement among proximate policymakers that feasible plans offer options but not full solutions. Reform in public welfare is apt to be incremental and based upon tactical considerations. In our society, work is to be preferred to direct income subsidy, and this social dictum would appear applicable to family policy too. Government programs directed to "full employment" would seem to be compatible with family need.

Among the self-supporting, it is questionable that present government tax policies are sufficiently supportive of the family, and sometimes they create disincentives to formal family experience.[12] Other income-related governmental policies may also require revision. It is well-known, for example, that Social Security programs tend to discourage formal marriage among the elderly. These disincentives to family experience, created by government, are subject to direct remedy through policy change.

HEALTH

The health delivery system should be integrated and should offer improved family-oriented services. Family health policy may be considered one aspect of income policy. A large number of subsidized health proposals for the nation have been devised, and many carry the promise of insuring against financial catastrophe as a result of illness. In fact, the present Medicaid and Medicare programs are ultimately compensations for expenditures for health services based upon public assistance and insurance models respectively. The desirability of protecting families against poverty and indigence has been indicated, and in this sense national health plans provide further protection.

But there is quite another perspective on the question of health reform in the United States. Many of the programs now being proposed contain within them efforts to regulate and change the organization of health-related services. Indeed, current experiments in comprehensive health planning and professional peer review are steps toward attempted control of health delivery systems. The health industry has become a subject for public policy. From the viewpoint of the family, however, health delivery in the United States is relatively backward.

Against a backdrop of rising concern about the cost of medical care and a growing conviction that aspects of the medical delivery system will require higher levels of public support, efforts to expand the health delivery system may be resisted. The family orientation could be seen as increasing costs unnecessarily and overburdening the system by adding a new component for professional concern and activity. Cost effectiveness demonstrations might be required to illustrate the efficiency of including the total family.

The National Research Council, in its family policy recommendations, describes the family as carrying the "pivotal role" with relation to child health. It states:

> Because the family is primarily responsible for child rearing in the United States, the prevention of social, psychological, and physical illness in children is best accomplished in the family context. Prevention of illness for children should include the promotion of good health for adults in the family, because, when adult family members suffer from ill health, the needs of children are often neglected.[13]

The matter gains in significance as the report considers the relationship between families afflicted by poverty and racism and the serious problems of infant mortality (the United States stood sixteenth among nations in this regard in 1975), the extreme disparities in accessibility to health service, the inadequacies of immunization programs, and the poor record in preventing disabilites.[14]

It is not difficult to imagine how the family could become involved in processes to improve American health care. A family-oriented health delivery approach not only might make the family less vulnerable to serious disturbances but also might engage it in more effective provision of health care. Health service delivery is likely to be more effective in team practice than through an entrepreneurial physician system. The health delivery team can usefully enlarge its professional ranks and even form links with other nonmedical community resources. Methods to promote the equity of medical care throughout the nation, such as expanded third-party payments, would enhance family life. And human relations skills could well be stressed more fully in medical, paramedical, and ancillary training.

SERVICE INTEGRATION

Administrative structures need to be designed which control family-oriented services of various kinds provided by multiple organizations. These structures must make possible rational administration, serve the peculiar purposes of the individual human service situation, and seek and utilize citizens' input. Policies that enlarge both public and voluntary services to families have been considered. A consideration of comprehensive policy development leads naturally into the subject of comprehensive program administration. Although there has been a trend toward umbrella administration in human service planning, including the use of multiple service providers, the efficiency and effectiveness of such designs is in considerable doubt.[15] These emerging service designs tend to be organized to stress accountability by service providers to the umbrella administration and in some instances give too little attention to service.

Appropriate administrative designs have not been sufficiently developed in the human services, and there is particular weakness in programming for family need. In general, the administrative goals for comprehensive services have far outrun the capacity to provide services comprehensively or to involve communities in their development so that they become an integral part of American organizational culture. With the necessity for developing pluralistic programs the capacity to administer complex program components becomes particularly important. Furthermore, the concept of services to families cuts across many other program interests and, therefore, such service designs can be expected to compete with other ways of defining service needs. Admittedly, administrative arrangements are a particularly weak element in the move toward family policy. Model development and testing through demonstration programs will be required. Such program demonstration has been suggested as one purpose of a central family bureau, and demonstrations geared toward providing comprehensive family services in localities, using pluralistic designs and seeking more family input, would seem to be in order. Moreover, the question of administrative layers also should be addressed. Some program elements can best be provided through centralized planning and funding on a national basis (public assistance, national health insurance, most aspects of research and demonstration). Others will require local approaches—the personal services such as counseling, education, and direct care programs. One can foresee the eventual development of a federal-state-local structure, with certain services reserved to different levels of government and to private activity. As this develops, it will be important to retain a sensitivity to administrative accountability, to the conditions necessary for providing good direct services, and to citizen interest.

THE STRATEGIC OUTLOOK

As has been noted throughout this book, a public consensus in support of a specific national family policy has not yet emerged. For this reason any consideration of strategy is necessarily difficult. The actors are diverse—private and public figures, organizational representatives and individuals, tightly formed organizations and vaguely defined social movements. Much strategy has been discussed, including such matters as the need for interest groups to coalesce and to engage in a "play of power"; the need to establish preconditions and a critical mass for policy development; and the need to develop metapolicy positions as guidelines for detailed policy development.

But what of establishing a single comprehensive national family policy for the United States? Enactment of such a policy seems extremely distant. Instead, the current scene offers some promise that several comprehensive views of family policy may evolve from many quarters. For example, departments of government, interest groups, and academic and research settings are becoming involved with policy development. Family interests, long buried within ancillary causes, seem to be demanding increasing attention. The idea that there is legitimate public concern with the family requires a reversal of both long-standing public attitudes and government indifference. One might expect a concern with macropolicy to surface from many quarters over many years before an American consensus has evolved, and an explicit and meaningful national family policy is possible. In another sense, however, macropolicy forms as interest is expressed in it. The family becomes a cause because it is expressed as such!

The author has discussed the barriers to policy development created by American views of individualism and privacy and the need to develop information on how government already has an impact on the family to dispel the myth that the family can be removed from public affairs. There is also the need to demonstrate that government activity in support of the family does not demand control and regulation of individual family experience and that it can support the rich pluralism that is so much a part of the American experience.

To establish a macropolicy on the family for the American government poses problems derived from increased salience and consequent conflict, the nature of existing law, and, ultimately, a degree of political consensus that seems unlikely in the near term. What is more likely is that a sense of implicit macropolicy may well begin to permeate the activities of government and structures surrounding it as individual components of policy come to the fore and as versions of explicit policy by proximate policymakers become known. At state and local levels, these components may be expressed in family law, welfare administration, health services development, mental health programming, and private human service activity. At the national level, broader knowledge of the family could have great impact, while such program activities as national health insurance, welfare reform, consideration of allied services programs, and tax reform might include increasing debate on some of the metapolicy issues discussed here. Those interested in the family are going to need to find ways to articulate their concerns with reference to many specific activities that may be foreseen as government priorities.

In 1962, Michael Harrington's study of poverty, *The Other America*, was published.[16] The book gained popularity among those in government, as well as the public at large, and made Americans considerably more aware of one major social problem in their midst. Subsequently, very specific government programs directed toward the alleviation of poverty were mounted and a period of great activity was under way. Today, American awareness of the family as a social issue is similar to the awareness of poverty in the early 1960s. This is a time for introducing the family as a legitimate concern of public policy. Its importance transcends that of many other social concerns. It is reasonable that the attention directed to the family be commensurate with its critical position in determining the nature of life in the United States.

NOTES

1. Monique de Bats Denis, Maurice Arfeux, Ype Schaaf, and Hermann Schubnell, Report of the Group of Four (Paris: International Union of Family Organizations, January 1976).

2. George Peter Murdock, The Universality of the Nuclear Family, in *A Modern Introduction to the Family*, eds. Norman W. Bell and Ezra F. Vogel (New York: The Free Press, 1968), pp. 37-44.

3. For example, several articles dealing with this subject may be found in Bell and Vogel, *A Modern Introduction to the Family*, pp. 37-112.

4. Robert F. Winch, *The Modern Family* (New York: Holt, Rinehart and Winston, 1971), p. 634.

5. Virginia Yan McLaughlin, Patterns of Work and Family Organization: Buffalo's Italians, in *The American Family in Sociocultural Perspective*, ed. Michael Gordon (New York: St. Martin's Press, 1973), pp. 136-48.

6. John McKnight, Colloquium on the Family. Paper presented the annual meeting of the Central and Midwest Regional Councils of Family Service Association of America, Chicago, 29 March 1976.

7. Bell and Vogel, *A Modern Introduction to the Family*, pp. 9-20.

8. *Ibid.*, pp. 1-34.

9. William F. Ogburn, with the assistance of Clark Tibbitts, The Family and Its Functions, in The President's Research Committee on Social Trends, *Recent Social Trends in the United States* (New York: Whittlesey House, 1934), pp. 661-708.

10. A current and popular example of this genre by a well-regarded marriage counselor states, "Open Family Living is a way of living together that offers new hope to families dissatisfied with the failures and limitations of the older styles. It is more flexible than living styles of the past. It puts stronger emphasis on respecting the uniqueness of each person, recognizing his feelings and

needs, and encouraging the development of personal, marital, and family potentials. It is *not* an approach based on conformity to rigid rules and fixed positions." Thomas C. McGinnis and John U. Ayres, *Open Family Living* (Garden City, N.Y.: Doubleday, 1976), p. 7.

11. Marc Sheinbein, Normal Crises: Stage Theory and Family Therapy, *Journal of Family Counseling*, Spring 1976, pp. 78-83.

12. Jo Richard Udry, *The Social Context of Marriage* (Philadelphia: J. B. Lippincott Co., 1966), p. 18.

13. Bell and Vogel, *A Modern Introduction to the Family*, pp. 7-9.

14. Marvin B. Sussman, Family Systems in the 1970's: Analysis, Policies and Programs, *The Annals of the American Academy*, July 1971, p. 42.

15. *Ibid.*, p. 56.

16. Helen Frank, Feeling Happy, *Journal of Family Counseling*, Spring 1976, pp. 23-27.

17. Richard E. Farson, Behavioral Science Predicts and Projects, in *The Future of the Family*, eds. Richard E. Farson, Philip M. Hauser, Herbert Stroup, and Anthony J. Weiner (New York: Family Service Association of America, 1969), p. 59.

18. Roslyn Feldberg and Janet Kohen, Family Life in an Anti-Family Setting: A Critique of Marriage and Divorce, *The Family Coordinator*, April 1976, pp. 151-59.

19. For example, see John Bowlby, *Child Care and the Growth of Love* (New Britain, Conn.: Penguin Books, 1953).

20. Arthur C. Emlen, Historical Perspectives in Trends in Day Care. Paper presented at seminar on contemporary trends in day care, given at Center for Continuing Education and Community Action for Social Services, University of Wisconsin, 24 June 1974.

21. J. W. Getzels, Socialization and Education: A Note on Discontinuities, in *The Family as Educator*, ed. Hope Jensen Leichter (New York: Teachers College Press, 1974), pp. 45-51.

22. Daniel P. Moynihan, A Family Policy for the Nation, in *The Moynihan Report and the Politics of Controversy*, eds. Lee Rainwater and William L. Yancey (Cambridge, Mass.: The MIT Press, 1967).

23. Winch, *The Modern Family*, pp. 215-26.

24. *Ibid.*, pp. 227-28.

25. Bernard Farber, Bilateral Kinship: Centripetal and Centrifugal Types of Organizations, *Journal of Marriage and the Family*, November 1975, pp. 871-88.

26. Allan Schnaiberg and Sheldon Goldenberg, Closing the Circle: The Impact of Children on Parental Status, *Journal of Marriage and the Family*, November 1975, pp. 937-53.

27. William J. Goode, *The Family* (Englewood Cliffs, N.J.: Prentice Hall, 1965), p. 50.

28. *Ibid.*, p. 55.

29. Talcott Parsons and Renee C. Fox, Illness, Therapy, and the Modern Urban American Family, in Bell and Vogel, *A Modern Introduction to the Family*, pp. 377-90.

30. Goode, *The Family*, p. 110.

31. Rosabeth Moss Kanter has produced an excellent literature survey detailing how families interact with work settings in her book, *Work and Family in the United States: A Critical Overview and Agenda for Research and Policy* (New York: Russell Sage Foundation, 1977).

32. Sussman, Family Systems in the 1970's, pp. 46-48.

33. *Ibid.*, p. 47.

34. *Ibid.*, p. 48.

35. Bell and Vogel, *A Modern Introduction to the Family*, pp. 9-20.

36. Peter A. Moock, Economic Aspects of the Family as Educator, in Leichter, *The Family as Educator*, pp. 92-97.

37. *Ibid.*, p. 96.

38. Bell and Vogel, *A Modern Introduction to the Family*, pp. 11-14.

39. John Scanzoni, *The Conjugal Family and Consumption Behavior* (Bryn Mawr: The McCahan Foundation, 1968).

40. M. Geraldine Gage, Economic Roles of Wives and Family Economic Development, *Journal of Marriage and the Family*, February 1975, pp. 121-28.

41. Christopher Lasch, The Family and History, *The New York Review of Books*, 13 November 1975, p. 33.

42. *Ibid.*, pp. 33-38; Christopher Lasch, The Emotions of Family Life, *The New York Review of Books*, 27 November 1975, pp. 37-42; and Christopher Lasch, What the Doctor Ordered, *The New York Review of Books*, 11 December 1975, pp. 50-54.

43. Peter Laslett, *The World We Have Lost* (New York: Charles Scribner's Sons, 1971), pp. 100-104.

44. Edward Shorter, *The Making of the Modern Family* (New York: Basic Books, 1975), pp. 175-76.

45. Barbara Laslett, The Family as a Public and Private Institution: A Historical Perspective, *Journal of Marriage and the Family*, August 1973, p. 480.

46. Susan L. Norton, Marital Migration in Essex County, Massachu-

setts, in the Colonial and Early Federal Periods, *Journal of Marriage and the Family*, August 1973, pp. 406-18.

47. Philippe Aries, *Centuries of Childhood* (New York: Knopf, 1962).

48. Shorter, *The Making of the Modern Family*, pp. 175-76.

49. Daniel Scott Smith, Parental Power and Marriage Patterns: An Analysis of Historical Trends in Hingham, Massachusetts, *Journal of Marriage and the Family*, August 1973, pp. 419–28.

50. Barbara Laslett, The Family as a Public and Private Institution, p. 487.

51. Shorter, *The Making of the Modern Family*, p. 244.

52. *Ibid.*, p. 254.

chapter 2

1. Abbott L. Ferriss, *Indicators of Change in the American Family* (New York: Russell Sage Foundation, 1970).

2. Bertram S. Brown, How Women See Their Roles: A Change in Attitudes, *New Dimensions in Mental Health*, September 1976.

3. *Data Track Women* (New York: New York Institute of Life Insurance, Summer 1974), p. 5.

4. U.S. Bureau of the Census, *Statistical Abstract of the U.S.: '75* (Washington: U.S. Government Printing Office, 1975), p. 34.

5. *Data Track Women*, p. 9.

6. *Ibid.*, p. 8.

7. Yankelovich, Skelly, and White, Inc., *The General Mills American Family Report 1974-75* (Minneapolis: General Mills, Inc., 1975), p. 32.

8. *Ibid.*, p. 31.

9. Dorothy Fahs Beck, *Marriage and the Family Under Challenge: An Outline of Issues, Trends, and Alternatives* (New York: Family Service Association of America, 1976), p. 12.

10. Trends in Expected Family Size in the United States, *Metropolitan Life Statistical Bulletin*, January 1975, pp. 10-11.

11. Beck, *Marriage and the Family* . . ., p. 12.

12. Estimates by Christopher Tietze, quoted in Beck, *ibid.*, p. 13.

13. Michael Novak, The Family Out of Favor, *Harper's Magazine*, April 1976, pp. 37-46.

14. Paul C. Glick, *Some Recent Changes in American Families*, Special Studies Series P-23, No. 52 (Washington: U.S. Government Printing Office, 1975), p. 2.

15. Jessie Bernard, Notes on Changing Lifestyles, *Journal of Marriage and the Family*, August 1975, p. 584.

16. *Household and Family Characteristics: Current Population Reports* (Washington: U.S. Government Printing Office, February 1976), Series P-20, No. 291, p. 2.

17. Recent Marriage and Divorce Trends Continuing, *HUD Newsletter*, 31 May 1976, p. 1.

18. Glick, *Some Recent Changes . . .*, pp. 4-5.

19. Census Finds Adults Wed Later, Divorce Sooner, *The New York Times*, 8 January 1976, p. 62.

20. *Data Track Women*, p. 19.

21. Beck, *Marriage and the Family . . .*, p. 11.

22. Glick, *Some Recent Changes . . .*, p. 10.

23. *Ibid.*, p. 6.

24. Paul C. Glick and Arthur J. Norton, quoted in Beck, *Marriage and the Family . . .*, p. 11.

25. Census Finds Adults Wed Late, Divorce Sooner, p. 62.

26. Margie Casady, quoted in Beck, *Marriage and the Family . . .*, p. 14.

27. Glick and Norton, quoted in Beck, *Marriage and the Family . . .*, p. 24.

28. Heather L. Ross and Isabel V. Sawhill, *Time of Transition* (Washington: The Urban Institute, 1975), p. 160.

29. *Data Track Women*, pp. 14-16.

30. Bernard, Notes on Changing Lifestyles, p. 585.

31. Beck, *Marriage and the Family . . .*, p. 11.

32. *HUD Newsletter*, 31 May 1976, p. 1.

33. A helpful brief summary of the nature of disagreement in the literature is available in William Ryan, *Blaming the Victim* (New York: Pantheon Books, 1971), pp. 61-85.

34. Glick, *Some Recent Changes . . .*, p. 13.

35. *Ibid.*, pp. 9-10.

36. Lucille Duberman, *The Reconstituted Family* (Chicago: Nelson-Hall Publishers, 1975).

37. Angus Campbell, Philip E. Converse, and Willard L. Rogers,

The Quality of American Life (New York: Russell Sage Foundation, 1976), p. 232.

38. Beck, *Marriage and the Family* . . ., p. 12.
39. Paul C. Glick, A Demographer Looks at American Families, *Journal of Marriage and the Family*, February 1975, p. 16.
40. Extracted from Herbert Bienstock, Recent Economic Trends and Their Implications for Urban Policy. Remarks before the Conference on a National Policy for Urban America, 21 May 1976. Data notes, p. 11.
41. Glick, *Some Recent Changes* . . ., p. 3.
42. *Data Track Women*, p. 18.
43. Glick, *Some Recent Changes* . . ., p. 13.
44. Bernard, Notes on Changing Lifestyles, p. 44.
45. Beck, *Marriage and the Family* . . ., p. 13.
46. Harold Edrich, ed., *Selected Findings from National Surveys* (New York: Institute of Life Insurance, Spring 1974), p. 7.
47. *Ibid.*, p. 11.
48. Yankelovich, *et al.*, *The General Mills American Family Report 1974-5*, p. 55.
49. Brown, How Women See Their Roles . . . .
50. Campbell, *et al.*, *The Quality of American Life*, p. 340.
51. *Ibid.*, p. 345.
52. *Ibid.*, p. 343.
53. Yankelovich, *et al.*, *The General Mills American Family Report 1974-75*, p. 97.
54. Barbara Everitt Bryant, Susan B. Evans, and Josephine Powell, *American Women in International Women's Year* (Detroit: Market Opinion Research, 1975), pp. 127-28.
55. Paul E. Mott, *Foster Care and Adoptions: Some Key Policy Issues* (Washington: U.S. Government Printing Office, 1975), p. 7.
56. Katherine Dickinson, Child Care, in *Five Thousand American Families—Patterns of Economic Progress*, vol. 3, eds. Greg J. Duncan and James N. Morgan (Ann Arbor, Michigan: Institute for Social Research, the University of Michigan, 1975), p. 222.
57. Gisela Konopka, *Young Girls: A Portrait of Adolescence* (Englewood Cliffs, N.J.: Prentice-Hall, 1976), p. 74.
58. Yankelovich, Skelly, and White, Inc., *The General Mills American Family Report 1976-77* (Minneapolis: General Mills. Inc., 1977).
59. Konopka, *Young Girls* . . . , p. 72.

60. Bryant, *et al.*, *American Women . . .* , p. 38.
61. Campbell *et al.*, *The Quality of American Life*, pp. 339-42.
62. Dickinson, Child Care, p. 224.
63. Computed from *American Families, Trends and Pressures, 1973* (Washington: U.S. Government Printing Office, 1974), p. 41.
64. Yankelovich, *et al.*, *The General Mills American Family Report 1974-75*, p. 47.
65. *Ibid.*, p. 62.
66. *Ibid.*, p. 93.
67. *Ibid.*, p. 59.
68. *Ibid.*, p. 60.
69. *Ibid.*, p. 99.

chapter 3

1. Charles E. Lindblom, *The Policy-Making Process* (Englewood Cliffs, N.J.: Prentice-Hall, 1958), pp. 28-42.
2. Reuben L. Hill, Challenges and Resources for Family Development. Paper presented at the Biennial Conference of Family Service Association of America, Detroit, Michigan, 12 November 1965, pp. 11-13.
3. Kenneth Borelli, The Implications of the New Ethnicity for American Social Work, *International Social Work*, April 1975, p. 7.
4. David and Vera Mace, *We Can Have Better Marriages If We Really Want Them* (Nashville: Abingdon Press, 1974), pp. 127-30.
5. John M. Romanyshyn, *Social Welfare: Charity to Justice* (New York: Random House, 1971), p. 339.
6. Daniel P. Moynihan, *The Politics of a Guaranteed Income* (New York: Vintage Books, 1973), pp. 24-25.
7. Harold L. Lurie, ed., *Encyclopedia of Social Work* (New York: National Association of Social Workers, 1965), p. 941.
8. Margaret E. Rich, *A Belief in People* (New York: Family Service Association of America, 1956), p. 94.

9. *Ibid.*, pp. 37-54.

10. Patrick V. Riley, The Family Service System: Unity Within Diversity. Paper presented at the Biennial Conference of Family Service Association of America, Boston, Massachusetts, 27 October 1975.

11. Edmund A. Sherman, Michael H. Phillips, Barbara L. Haring, and Ann W. Shyne, *Services to Children in Their Own Homes: Its Nature and Outcome* (New York: Child Welfare League of America, 1974).

12. *Ibid.*, pp. 4, 5.

13. Karl L. Swain, Marriage and Family Counselor Licensure: Special Reference to Nevada, *Journal of Marriage and Family Counseling*, April 1975, p. 149.

14. *Ibid.*

15. Meyer Elkin, Licensing Marriage and Family Counselors: A Model Act, *Journal of Marriage and Family Counseling*, July 1975, p. 242.

16. William H. Blanchard, Encounter Group and Society, in *New Perspectives on Encounter Groups*, eds. Lawrence N. Solomon and Betty Berzon (San Francisco: Jossey-Bass, Inc., 1972), pp. 13-14.

17. Leonard D. Borman, ed., *Explorations in Self-Help and Mutual Aid* (Evanston, Ill.: Center for Urban Affairs, Northwestern University, 1975), p.v.

18. Herbert A. Otto, *Marriage and Family Enrichment: New Perspectives and Programs* (Nashville: Abingdon Press, 1976), pp. 12-13.

19. Bruce M. Pringle, Family Clusters as a Means of Reducing Isolation Among Urbanites, *The Family Coordinator*, April 1974, pp. 175-79.

20. James W. Ramey, Intimate Networks: Will They Replace the Monogamous Family?, *The Futurist*, August 1975, pp. 175-81.

21. Brian O'Connell, The Contribution of Voluntary Agencies in Developing Social Policies. Paper presented at the Sidney Hollander Colloquium, Council of Jewish Federations and Welfare Funds, Chicago, 24-25 April 1976.

22. James L. Feldesman and Lawrence I. Hewes, Issues and Problems Associated with the Administration of Federal Financial Assistance Programs by Non-Profit, Voluntary Social Service Organizations. Report of the United Way of America.

23. One interesting example of the considerable literature criticizing

health care delivery is Arnold I. Kisch, The Health Care System and Health: Some Thoughts on a Famous Misalliance, *Inquiry*, December 1974, pp. 269-75.

24. Henrik L. Blum, *Planning for Health* (New York: Human Sciences Press, 1974), pp. 77–92.

25. Kisch, The Health Care System . . . , p. 273.

26. Lynn P. Carmichael, Family Medicine, in *Family Health Care*, eds. Debra P. Hymovich and Martha Underwood Bernard (New York: McGraw-Hill, 1973), p. 61.

27. William G. Hill, Joseph B. Lehmann, and Elizabeth J. Slotkin, *Family Service Agencies and Mental Health Clinics* (New York: Family Service Association of America, 1971).

28. Joint Commission on Mental Health of Children, *Crisis in Child Mental Health—Challenge for the 1970's* (New York: Harper and Row, 1970), p. 179.

29. Bertram S. Brown, The Crisis in Mental Health Research. Paper presented at the annual meeting of the American Psychiatric Association, Miami Beach, Florida, 13 May 1976.

30. Eleanor Hannon Judah, Public Social Policy and the Developmental Years, *Social Thought*, Summer 1976, p. 66.

31. Howard Oberheu, The Typical Family Compared with the AFDC Family, *Social and Rehabilitation Record*, July/August 1976, p. 6.

32. *Ibid.*, p. 8.

33. Judah, Public Social Policy . . . ,pp. 66-67.

34. Paul E. Mott, *Foster Care and Adoptions: Some Key Policy Issues* (Washington: U.S. Government Printing Office, 1975).

35. *Ibid.*, p. 6.

36. *Ibid.*, p. 11.

37. *Ibid.*, p. 14.

38. *Ibid.*, p. 15.

39. *Ibid.*, pp. 16-17.

40. *Ibid.*, p. 17.

41. *Ibid.*, pp. 18-19.

42. *Ibid.*, p. 31.

43. Geraldine M. Spark and Elaine M. Brody, The Aged Are Family Members, *Family Process*, September 1970, pp. 195-208.

44. U.S. Children's Bureau, Adoption Outline, Goal #3, pp. 2-3.

45. See *Building Blocks of Society*, brochure of the Young Men's Christian Association.

46. William F. Ogburn, The Changing Functions of the Family, in

Selected Studies in Marriage and the Family, eds. Robert F. Winch and Louis Wolf Goodman (New York: Holt, Rinehart and Winston, Inc., 1968), p. 59.

47. American Federation of Teachers' Executive Council, *Early-Childhood Education: A National Program* (Washington: American Federation of Teachers, AFL-CIO, item no. 620, 17 December 1974).

48. Testimony of Marian Wright Edelman on the Child and Family Services Act, *Congressional Record*, 22 February 1975, p. 524–28.

49. Arthur C. Emlen, Realistic Planning for The Day Care Consumer, in *Social Work Practice, 1970* (New York: Columbia University Press, 1970), pp. 127-42; and Slogans, Slots, and Slander: The Myth of Day Care Need, *American Journal Of Orthopsychiatry*, January 1973, pp. 23-36.

50. John Kenneth Galbraith, *The New Industrial State* (New York: Signet Books, 1967), pp. 176-88.

51. E. Jerry Walker, 'Til Business Us Do Part?, *Harvard Business Review*, January-February 1976, pp. 94-101.

52. Leo Perlis, The Human Contract in the Work Place, *Family Service Highlights*, September-October 1976, pp. 5-6.

53. The interplay of government and industry in providing family-oriented services in Europe is described in Alfred J. Kahn and Sheila B. Kamerman, *Not For The Poor Alone* (Philadelphia: Temple University Press, 1975), pp. 18-48.

54. Several American church positions on various matters connected with the family are available in William H. Genne, *A Synoptic of Recent Denominational Statements on Sexuality*, Second Edition (New York: National Council of Churches, n.d.).

55. Daniel P. Moynihan, A Family Policy for The Nation, in *The Moynihan Report and the Politics of Controversy*, eds. Lee Rainwater and William L. Yancy (Cambridge, Massachusetts: The M.I.T. Press, 1967), p. 389.

56. Moynihan, *The Politics of a Guaranteed Income*, pp. 259-302.

57. Moynihan, A Family Policy for the Nation, p. 389.

58. See, for example, Andrew Billingsley, *Black Families in White America* (Englewood Cliffs, N.J.: Prentice-Hall, Inc., 1968), pp. 193-98.

59. Daniel P. Moynihan, *The Negro Family: The Case for National Action* (Washington: U.S. Department of Labor, Office of Planning and Research, March 1965), p. 1.

60. Robert B. Hill, The Strengths of Black Families, monograph developed for the National Urban League, 8 July 1971.
61. Betty Friedan, *The Feminine Mystique* (New York: W. W. Norton & Co., 1963).
62. Mace, *We Can Have Better Marriages. . .* , pp. 39-40.
63. Dorothy Fahs Beck and Emily Bradshaw, *Current Challenges to the Traditional Family and Some Newly Emerging Alternate Forms for Family Living* (New York: Family Service Association of America, 1972).
64. The New Life. Report by the Vanier Institute of the Family, Ottawa, Canada, 1975, p. 18.
65. *Ibid.*, p. 12.
66. Moynihan, *The Politics of a Guaranteed Income*, speaks to the intricacies of political modification that occurred as this bill moved through the political process.
67. *Ibid.*, p. 345.
68. Subcommittee on Children and Youth of the Committee on Labor and Public Welfare, U.S. Senate, *Background Materials Concerning the Child and Family Services Act, 1975*, S. 626 (Washington: U.S. Government Printing Office, 1976).
69. *Ibid.*, p. ix.
70. *Ibid.*, p. 17.
71. *Ibid.*, pp. 29-75.
72. Amitai Etzioni, *The Active Society* (New York: The Free Press, 1968), p. 108.

chapter 4

1. Catherine S. Chilman, American Families and National Policies. Paper presented at the 1967 Conference of the International Scientific Commission on the Family, Quebec, Canada, 1967.
2. Daniel P. Moynihan, Policy vs. Program in the '70's, *The Public Interest*, Summer 1970, pp. 90-100.
3. *Ibid.*, p. 91.
4. *Ibid.*, p. 93.

5. For example, a fascinating multi-factorial comparative analysis of 24 European nations, considering many components of family policy, is available in Veronica Stolte-Heiskanen, Family Needs and Societal Institutions: Potential Empirical Linkage Mechanisms, *Journal of Marriage and the Family*, November 1975, pp. 903-16.

An example of private and governmental association, unusual if not unheard of in North America, is described in International Union of Family Organizations, *IUFO Information*, August-December 1973, pp. 25-28.

6. Alfred J. Kahn and Sheila B. Kamerman, *Not For The Poor Alone* (Philadelphia: Temple University Press, 1975).

7. *Ibid.*, pp. x-xi.

8. International Union of Family Organizations, *IUFO Information*, p. 26.

9. *The Federal Constitution of the Swiss Confederation*, Article 34, Section 1. Unofficial translation.

10. G. Desmottes, Implications for Social Policy of Changing Family Needs: The Beginnings of a Family Policy in Europe, *European Seminar in Relation to Changing Family Needs, Arnhem, Netherlands, 16-26 April 1961* (Geneva: United Nations, 1962), pp. 126-33.

11. *Ibid.*, p. 129.

12. United Nations Secretariat, *Trends in Social Conditions and Policies in Europe, Working Paper I* (Geneva: United Nations, 1974) pp. 14-15.

13. Alfred J. Kahn and Sheila B. Kamerman, European Family Policy Currents: The Question of Families with Very Young Children. Preliminary draft of a working paper, October 1976, p. 8.

14. Friedrich Engels, Transformation of the Family, in *A Modern Introduction to the Family*, eds. Norman W. Bell and Ezra F. Vogel (New York: The Free Press, 1968), pp. 45-47.

15. H. Kent Geiger, The Fate of the Family in the Soviet Union: 1917-1944, in Bell and Vogel, *A Modern Introduction to the Family*, pp. 48-68.

16. Urie Bronfenbrenner, Soviet Methods in Character Education: Some Implications for Research, in *Learning About Politics*, ed. R. S. Sigel (New York: Random House, 1970), pp. 10-15.

17. John M. Romanyshyn, *Social Welfare: Charity to Justice* (New York: Random House, 1971), p. 339.

18. *Ibid.*, pp. 339-40.

19. Harold L. Wilensky and Charles N. Lebeaux, *Industrial Society and Social Welfare* (New York: Russell Sage Foundation, 1958), p. 65.

20. Henry Sumner Maine, *Ancient Law* (New York: Henry Holt and Co., 1888), p. 168.

21. Shirley Zimmerman, The Family and Its Relevance for Social Policy, *Social Casework*, November 1976, pp. 547-54.

22. Alvin L. Schorr. Family Values and Real Life, *Social Casework*, June 1976, pp. 397-404.

23. Janet Zollinger Giele, Family Values and Family Policy. Paper presented at 1976 Groves Conference on Marriage and Family, Kansas City, Missouri, 25 March 1976, p. 2.

24. Alva Myrdal, *Nation and Family* (Cambridge, Mass.: The M.I.T. Press, 1968), pp. xviii, 231.

25. For example, see Daniel P. Moynihan, *The Politics of a Guaranteed Income* (New York: Random House, 1973), or Reuben L. Hill, Challenges and Resources for Family Development. Paper presented at the Biennial Conference of Family Service Association of America, Detroit, Michigan, 12 November 1965, p. 12.

26. Robert Staples, Public Policy and the Changing Status of Black Families, *The Family Coordinator*, July 1973.

27. Andrew Billingsley, Toward a National Family Policy, in *American Families: Trends and Pressures, 1973*, Committee on Labor and Public Welfare, U.S. Senate, (Washington: U.S. Government Printing Office, 1974), p. 309.

28. Romanyshyn, *Social Welfare. . .*, pp. 342–52.

29. Jessie Bernard, *The Future of Marriage* (New York: World Publishing, 1972), pp. 281-89.

30. Joan Aldous, The Intermingling of Governmental Policy, Social Structure and Family Values: The Case of the Changing Family, in *Social Policy and Sociology: Proceedings of a Conference on Policy Research and Graduate Training*, ed. N.F. Demerath (New York: Seminar Press, 1975), pp. 109-21.

31. Jacquelyne A. Gallop, Public School Policy and the Family Today, *Social Thought*, Winter 1976, pp. 43-54.

32. Amitai Etzioni, The Next Crisis: The End of the Family, *Evaluation*, January 1974, pp. 6-7.

33. Marvin B. Sussman, Family Systems in the 1970's: Analysis, Policies and Programs, *The Annals of the American Academy*, July 1971, pp. 40-56.

34. Schorr, Family Values . . . , pp. 397-404.

35. Urie Bronfenbrenner, Testimony Before the Senate Subcommittee on Children and Youth, in Committee on Labor and Public Welfare, *American Families* . . . , p. 147.

36. Bronfenbrenner, The Roots of Alienation, in *ibid.*, pp. 427-51.

37. Bronfenbrenner, The American Family Act of 1974: Suggested Principles and Provisions, in *ibid.*, pp. 172-77.

38. Mary Jo Bane, *Here to Stay* (New York: Basic Books, 1976).

39. *Ibid.*, p. 74.

40. Yehezkel Dror, *Public Policymaking Reexamined* (Scranton, Pa.: Chandler Publishing Co., 1968).

41. *Ibid.*, p. 8.

42. Zimmerman, The Family and Its Relevance . . . , pp. 547-54.

43. Sheila B. Kamerman and Alfred J. Kahn, Explorations in Family Policy, *Social Work*, May 1976, pp. 181-86.

44. *Ibid.*, p. 183.

45. For example, see Giele, Family Values . . . , or Helsinki Study Sessions of the International Union of Family Organizations, The Role of Public Authorities in the Development of the Whole of Family Policies. Report of the International Union of Family Organizations, Helsinki, Finland, 21-23 June 1976.

46. Norman V. Lourie, Presidential Address to the National Conference on Social Welfare. Paper presented at the National Conference on Social Welfare, Washington, D.C., 13-17 June 1976.

47. Subcommittee on Children and Youth of the Committee on Labor and Public Welfare, U.S. Senate, *Background Materials Concerning Child and Family Services Act, 1975*, S. 626. (Washington: U.S. Government Printing Office, 1976), p. ix.

48. *Ibid.*, pp. 24-27.

49. California Legislature, Assembly Bill 4302, *Family, Children and Parents Service Act, 1975-76 Regular Session*, 25 March 1976.

50. Florida Task Force on Marriage and the Family Unit, *Final Report* (Tallahassee: Florida State University Governmental Law Center and Institute for Social Research, May 1976).

51. Shriver Announces Comprehensive Program to Restore the Authority of American Families. News release, Des Moines, Iowa, Shriver for President, 15 January 1976.

52. Personal communication with Eunice Kennedy Shriver, 19 May 1976.

53. Joseph A. Califano, Jr., American Families: Trends, Pressures

and Recommendations. A preliminary report to Governor Jimmy Carter, 17 September 1976.

54. Jimmy Carter, speech to National Conference of Catholic Charities, Denver, Colorado, 4 October 1976.

55. Margaret Mead, Prepared Statement, Committee on Labor and Public Welfare, U.S. Senate, pp. 128-33.

56. Walter F. Mondale, A "Family Impact Statement"—A Response from the U.S. Senate, *School Review*, November 1974, pp. 11-14.

57. David Maxey, No More Messiahs, Please, *Psychology Today*, October 1974, p. 123, *passim*.

58. *Foundation for Child Development Annual Report: 1975-1976* (New York: Foundation for Child Development, 1976), pp. 13-14.

59. Sheila B. Kamerman, *Developing A Family Impact Statement* (New York: Foundation for Child Development, 1976).

60. Advisory Committee on Child Development, *Toward a National Policy for Children and Families* (Washington: National Academy of Sciences, 1976), p. vii.

61. *Ibid.*

62. *Ibid.*, p. 7.

chapter 5

1. Robert M. Rice, Impact of Government Contracts on Voluntary Social Agencies, *Social Casework*, July 1975, pp. 387-95; James L. Feldesman and Lawrence I. Hewes, Issues and Problems Associated with the Administration of Federal Financial Assistance Programs by Non-Profit, Voluntary Social Service Organizations. Report of the United Way of America.

2. Gordon Manser and Rosemary Higgins Cass, *Voluntarism at the Crossroads* (New York: Family Service Association of America, 1976), pp. 39-49.

134

American Family Policy

3. Yehezkel Dror, *Public Policymaking Reexamined* (Scranton, Pa.: Chandler Publishing Co., 1968).
4. Advisory Committee on Child Development, *Toward a National Policy for Children and Families* (Washington: National Academy of Sciences, 1976), p. 65.
5. There is much clinical literature from the mental health field on this topic. One major summation is contained in Joint Commission on Mental Health and Children, *Crisis in Child Mental Health: Challenge for the 1970's* (New York: Harper and Row, 1970), pp. 313-29.
6. Brian O'Connell, Voluntary Agencies Must Ask: What Price Independence?, *Foundation News*, July/August 1976, pp. 16-20.
7. For an interesting survey of contract devices which have evolved in defense procurement, see Raymond G. Hunt, R & D Management and Award Fee Contracting, *Journal of the Society of Research Administrators*, Summer 1974, pp. 33-44.
8. "Alert" Article Draws Industry Response, *Family Service Highlights April 1974*, pp. 3-4.
9. Earl W. Morris and Mary Winter, A Theory of Family Housing Adjustment, *Journal of Marriage and the Family*, February 1975, pp. 79-88.
10. Hilda Kahne, Women's Roles in the Economy, in *Economic Independence for Women*, ed. Jane Roberts Chapman (Beverly Hills: Sage Publications, 1976), pp. 39-76.
11. For example, see Blanche Bernstein and William Meezan, *The Impact of Welfare on Family Stability* (New York: Center for New York City Affairs, New School for Social Research, June 1975), or Howard Oberheu, The Typical Family Compared with the AFDC Family, *Social and Rehabilitation Review*, July/August 1976, pp. 6-8.
12. For example, see Statement of Dr. Harvey E. Brazer, Professor of Economics and Research Associate, Institute of Policy Studies, University of Michigan, in Committee on Labor and Public Welfare, U.S. Senate, *American Families: Trends and Pressures, 1973* (Washington: U.S. Government Printing Office, 1974), pp. 204-13.
13. Advisory Committee for Children and Families, *Toward a National Policy . . .* , p. 55.
14. *Ibid.*, pp. 55-64.
15. For a more detailed discussion, see Robert M. Rice, A Cau-

tionary View of Allied Services, *Social Casework*, April 1977, pp. 229-35.

16. Michael Harrington, *The Other America* (New York: Macmillan Co., 1962).

BIBLIOGRAPHY

"A Conversation with William C. Nichols, Jr., Ed.D." **Marriage, Divorce and Family Newsletter,** December, 1976, p. 2.

Advisory Committee on Child Development. **Toward A National Policy for Children and Families.** Washington, D.C.: National Academy of Sciences, 1976.

Aldous, Joan. "The Intermingling of Governmental Policy, Social Structure and Family Values: The Case of the Changing Family." In **Social Policy and Sociology: Proceedings of a Conference on Policy Research and Graduate Training,** edited by N.F. Demerath. New York: Seminar Press, 1975.

" 'Alert' Article Draws Industry Response." **Family Service Highlights,** 4:3-4 (April 1974).

American Federation of Teachers' Executive Council. **Early Childhood Education: A National Program.** Washington, D.C.: American Federation of Teachers, AFL-CIO. Item No. 620, 17 December 1974.

Aries, Philippe. **Centuries of Childhood.** New York: Alfred A. Knopf, 1962.

Association of Couples for Marriage Enrichment. Press release. Winston-Salem, N.C., 24 November 1976.

Bane, Mary Jo. **Here To Stay.** New York: Basic Books, 1976.

Beck, Dorothy Fahs. **Marriage and the Family Under Challenge: An Outline of Issues, Trends, and Alternatives.** New York: Family Service Association of America, 1976.

_____, and Bradshaw, Emily. **Current Challenges to the Traditional Family and Some Newly Emerging Alternate Forms for Family Living.** New York: Family Service Association of America, 1972.

Becker, Gary S. "A Theory of Marriage: Part I." **Journal of Political Economy,** 81: 813-46 (July/August, 1973).

_____. "A Theory of Marriage: Part II." In "Marriage, Family Human Capital and Fertility," Theodore W. Schultz. Supplement to **Journal of Political Economy**, part 2, 82:11–26 (March/April 1974).

_____. "A Theory of the Allocation of Time." **The Economic Journal**, 16:493–517 (September 1965).

Bell, Norman W., and Vogel, Ezra F., eds. **A Modern Introduction to the Family.** New York: The Free Press, 1968.

Bernard, Jessie. "Notes on Changing Lifestyles." **Journal of Marriage and the Family**, 37:582-93 (August 1975).

_____. **The Future of Marriage.** New York: World Publishing, 1972.

Bernstein, Blanche, and Meezan, William. **The Impact of Welfare on Family Stability.** New York: Center for New York City Affairs, New School for Social Research, June 1975.

Bienstock, Herbert. "Recent Economic Trends and Their Implications for Urban Policy." Remarks before the Conference on a National Policy for Urban America, New York, 21 May 1976.

Billingsley, Andrew. **Black Families in White America.** Englewood Cliffs, N.J.: Prentice-Hall, Inc., 1968.

_____. "The Evolution of the Black Family." **New York Amsterdam News, Special Bicentennial Edition**, Summer 1976, pp. A1-A3.

Blanchard, William H. "Encounter Group and Society." In **New Perspectives on Encounter Groups**, edited by Lawrence N. Solomon and Betty Berzon. San Francisco: Jossey-Bass, Inc., 1972.

Blum, Henrik L. **Planning for Health.** New York: Human Sciences Press, 1974.

Borelli, Kenneth. "The Implications of the New Ethnicity for American Social Work." **International Social Work**, 18:1-9 (April 1975).

Borman, Leonard D., ed. **Explorations in Self-Help and Mutual Aid.** Evanston, Ill.: Center for Urban Affairs, Northwestern University, 1975.

Bowlby, John. **Child Care and the Growth of Love.** New Britain, Conn.: Penguin Books, 1953.

Brier, Judith, and Rubenstein, Dan. "Sex for the Elderly?" **Perspective on Aging**, 5:5-10 (November/December 1976).

Brim, Orville G., Jr. "Macro-Structural Influences on Child Development and the Need for Childhood Social Indicators." **American Journal of Orthopsychiatry**, 45:516-24 (July 1975).

Bronfenbrenner, Urie. "Soviet Methods in Character Education: Some Implications for Research." In **Learning About Politics**, edited by R.S. Sigel. New York: Random House, 1970.

Brown, Bertram S. "How Women See Their Roles: A Change in Attitudes." **New Dimensions in Mental Health**, September 1976.

_____. "The Crisis in Mental Health Research." Paper presented at the Annual Meeting of the American Psychiatric Association, Miami Beach, Florida, 13 May 1976.

Bryant, Barbara Everitt; Evans, Susan B.; and Powell, Josephine. **American Women in International Women's Year.** Detroit, Mich.: Market Opinion Research, 1975.

Bunker, Douglas R. "Policy Sciences Perspectives on Implementation Processes." **Policy Sciences**, 3:71-80 (1972).

Califano, Joseph A., Jr. "American Families: Trends, Pressures and Recommendations." A preliminary report to Governor Jimmy Carter, 17 September 1976.

California Legislature Assembly Bill 4302. **Family, Children and Parents Service Act, 1975-76 Regular Session.** 25 March 1976.

Campbell, Angus; Converse, Philip E.; and Rogers, Willard L. **The Quality of American Life.** New York: Russell Sage Foundation. 1976.

Carmichael, Lynne P. "Family Medicine." In **Family Health Care**, edited by Debra P. Hymovich and Martha Underwood Bernard. New York: McGraw-Hill, 1973.

Carter, Jimmy. "Statement on the American Family." Speech given in Manchester, N.H., 3 August 1976.

_____. Untitled speech to National Conference of Catholic Charities, Denver, Colorado, 4 October 1976.

"Center for the Family." **Journal of Home Economics**, 67:64 (May 1974).

Chaganti, Radharao; Donohue, William; Nelson, Walter; Ruben, Mark; and Rice, Robert. **Guidelines for Development of a National Family**

Policy, Discussion Paper #9. Buffalo, N.Y.: Center for Policy Studies, State University of New York at Buffalo, n.d.

Chilman, Catherine S. "American Families and National Policies." Paper presented at the 1967 Conference of the International Commission on the Family, Quebec, Ontario, 1967.

Data Track Women. New York: Institute of Life Insurance, 1974.

Delbecq, Andre L., and Van de Ven, Andrew H. "A Group Process Model for Problem Indentification and Program Planning." Journal of Applied Behavioral Science, 7:466-92 (July 1971).

Denis, Monique de Bats; Arfeux, Maurice; Schaaf, Ype; and Schubnell, Hermann. "Report of the Group of Four." Report presented at the International Union of Family Organizations, Paris, January 1976.

Desmottes, George. "Implications for Social Policy of Changing Family Needs: The Beginnings of a Family Policy in Europe." In European Seminar in Relation to Changing Family Needs, Arnhem, Netherlands, 16-26 April 1961. Geneva: United Nations, 1962.

_____. "Legislative Provisions on the Institution of the Family: The Reciprocal Rights and Duties of Husband and Wife." In Young Families in the Society. Paris: International Union of Family Organizations, 1969.

Dickinson, Katherine. "Child Care." In Five Thousand American Families—Patterns of Economic Progress, vol. III, edited by Greg J. Duncan and James N. Morgan. Ann Arbor, Michigan: Institute for Social Research, University of Michigan, 1975.

Division of Information Systems and Services. Family Service Profiles: Agency Program and Funding: 1975. New York: Family Service Association of America, 1976.

Dror, Yehezkel. Public Policymaking Reexamined. Scranton, Pa.: Chandler Publishing Co., 1968.

Duberman, Lucille. The Reconstituted Family. Chicago: Nelson-Hall Publishers, 1975.

Duncan, Greg J., and Hill, C. Russell. "Modal Choice in Child Care Arrangements." In Five Thousand American Families—Patterns of Economic Progress, vol. III, edited by Greg J. Duncan and James N. Morgan. Ann Arbor, Michigan: Institute for Social Research, University of Michigan, 1975.

_____, and Newman, Sandra. "People as Planners: The Fulfillment of Residential Mobility Expectations." In **Five Thousand American Families—Patterns of Economic Progress**, vol. III, edited by Greg J. Duncan and James N. Morgan. Ann Arbor, Michigan: Institute for Social Research, University of Michigan, 1975.

Edrich, Harold, ed. **Selected Findings from National Surveys**. New York: Institute of Life Insurance, 1974.

Elkin, Meyer. "Licensing Marriage and Family Counselors: A Model Act." **Journal of Marriage and Family Counseling**, 1:237-49 (July 1975).

Emery, F.E., ed. **Systems Thinking**. Harmondsworth, Middlesex, England: Penguin Books, 1969.

Emlen, Arthur C. "Historical Perspectives in Trends in Day Care." Paper presented at a seminar on contemporary trends in day care at Center for Continuing Education and Community Action for Social Services, University of Wisconsin, 24 June 1974.

_____. "Realistic Planning for the Day Care Consumer." **Social Work Practice, 1970**. New York: Columbia University Press, 1970.

_____. "Slogans, Slots, and Slander: The Myth of Day Care Need." **American Journal of Orthopsychiatry**, 43:23-36 (January 1973).

Etzioni, Amitai. **The Active Society**. New York: The Free Press, 1968.

_____. "The Family Under Fire." **The Washington Post Outlook**, 28 December 1975, pp. A20-A21.

_____. "The Next Crisis: The End of the Family?" **Evaluation**, 2:6-7 (January 1974).

Family Research Unit. **The Australian Family**. Kensington, N.S.W., Australia: University of New South Wales, School of Social Work, 1975.

Farber, Bernard. "Bilateral Kinship: Centripetal and Centrifugal Types of Organizations." **Journal of Marriage and the Family**, 37:871-88 (November 1975).

Farson, Richard E.; Hauser, Philip M.; Stroup, Herbert; and Wiener, Anthony J. **The Future of the Family**. New York: Family Service Association of America, 1969.

Feldberg, Roslyn, and Kohen, Janet. "Family Life in an Anti-Family Setting: A Critique of Marriage and Divorce." **The Family Coordinator**, 25:151-59 (April 1976).

Feldesman, James L., and Hewes, Lawrence I. "Issues and Problems Associated with the Administration of Federal Financial Assistance Programs by Non-Profit, Voluntary Social Service Organizations." Report of the United Way of America, n.d.

Female Family Heads. Series P-23, No. 50. Washington, D.C.: U.S. Government Printing Office, 1974.

Ferriss, Abbott L. Indicators of Change in the American Family. New York: Russell Sage Foundation, 1970.

Florida Task Force on Marriage and the Family Unit. Final Report. Tallahassee: Florida State University Governmental Law Center and Institute for Social Research (May 1976).

Foundation for Child Development Annual Report: 1975-1976. New York: Foundation for Child Development, 1976.

Frank, Helen. "Feeling Happy." Journal of Family Counseling, 4:23-27 (Spring 1976).

Friedan, Betty. The Feminine Mystique. New York: W.W. Norton & Co., 1963.

Gage, M. Geraldine. "Economic Roles of Wives and Family Economic Development." Journal of Marriage and the Family, 37:121-28 (February 1975).

Galbraith, John Kenneth. The New Industrial State. New York: Signet Books, 1967.

Gallop, Jacquelyne A. "Public Social Policy and the Family Today." Social Thought, 2:43-54 (Winter 1976).

Genne, William H. A Synoptic of Recent Denominational Statements on Sexuality. 2nd ed. New York: National Council of Churches, n.d.

Giele, Janet Zollinger. "Family Values and Family Policy." Paper presented at the 1976 Groves Conference on Marriage and Family, Kansas City, Missouri, 25 March 1976.

Glick, Paul C. "A Demographer Looks at American Families." Journal of Marriage and the Family, 37:15-27 (February 1975).

_____. Some Recent Changes in American Families. Special Studies P-23, No. 52. Washington, D.C.: U.S. Government Printing Office, 1975.

Goldstein, Joseph; Freud, Anna; and Solnit, Albert J. **Beyond the Best Interests of the Child.** New York: The Free Press, 1973.

Goode, William J. **The Family.** Englewood Cliffs, N.J.: Prentice-Hall, 1965.

Gordon, Michael, and Hareven, Tamara. "Some Comments from the Guest Editors." **Journal of Marriage and the Family,** 35:393-94 (August 1973).

Groves Conference on Marriage and the Family. Conference program. Kansas City, Missouri, 25-27 March 1976.

Haggerty, Robert J. "The Conceptual and Empirical Bases of Family Health Care." In **Family Health Care: Health Promotion and Illness Care,** edited by Robert C. Jackson and Jean Morton. Berkeley, California: School of Public Health, University of California, 1976.

Harrington, Michael. **The Other America.** New York: The Macmillan Co., 1962.

Helsinki Study Sessions of the International Union of Family Organizations. "The Role of Public Authorities in the Development of the Whole of Family Policies." Report of the International Union of Family Organizations, Helsinki, Finland, 21-23 June 1976.

Hill, Reuben L. "Challenges and Resources for Family Development." Paper presented at the Biennial Conference of Family Service Association of America, Detroit, Michigan, 12 November 1965.

Hill, Robert B. "The Strengths of Black Families." Monograph developed for the National Urban League, 8 July 1971.

Hill, William G.; Lehmann, Joseph B.; and Slotkin, Elizabeth J. **Family Service Agencies and Mental Health Clinics.** New York: Family Service Association of America, 1971.

Household and Family Characteristics: Current Population Reports. Series P-20, No. 291. Washington, D.C.: U.S. Government Printing Office, February 1976.

Hunt, Raymond G. "R & D Management and Award Fee Contracting." **Journal of the Society of Research Administrators,** 6:33-40 (Summer 1974).

International Union of Family Organizations. **IUFO Information,** 25-28 (August-December 1973).

Joint Commission on Mental Health of Children. **Crisis in Child Mental Health—Challenge for the 1970s.** New York: Harper and Row, 1970.

Judah, Eleanor Hannon. "Public Social Policy and the Developmental Years." **Social Thought,** 2:63-70 (Summer 1976).

Kahn, Alfred J., and Kamerman, Sheila B. "European Family Policy Currents: The Question of Families with Very Young Children." Preliminary draft of a working paper, October 1976.

_____. "Government and the Family in the U.S." Preliminary draft of a working paper, Columbia Uinversity School of Social Work, February 1977.

_____. **Not For The Poor Alone.** Philadelphia: Temple University Press, 1975.

Kahne, Hilda. "Women's Roles in the Economy." In **Economic Independence for Women,** edited by Jane Roberts Chapman. Beverly Hills: Sage Publications, 1976.

Kamerman, Sheila B. **Developing a Family Impact Statement.** New York: Foundation for Child Development, 1976.

_____, and Kahn, Alfred J. "Explorations in Family Policy." **Social Work,** 21:181-86 (May 1976).

Kanter, Rosabeth Moss. **Work and Family in the United States: A Critical Review and Agenda for Research and Policy.** New York: Russell Sage Foundation, 1977.

Kisch, Arnold I. "The Health Care System and Health: Some Thoughts on a Famous Misalliance." **Inquiry,** 11:269-75 (December 1974).

Konopka, Gisela. "Adolescent Girls: A Two-Year Study." **Center Quarterly,** 1-7 (Fall 1976).

_____. **Young Girls: A Portrait of Adolescence.** Englewood Cliffs, N.J.: Prentice-Hall, Inc., 1976.

Land, Kenneth C., and Spilerman, Seymour. **Social Indicator Models.** New York: Russell Sage Foundation, 1975.

Lasch, Christopher. "The Emotions of Family Life." **The New York Review of Books,** 27 November 1975, pp. 37-42.

_____. "The Family and History." **The New York Review of Books,** 13 November 1975, pp. 33-38.

_____. "What the Doctor Ordered." **The New York Review of Books,** 11 December 1975, pp. 50-54.

Laslett, Barbara. "The Family as a Public and Private Institution: An Historical Perspective." **Journal of Marriage and the Family,** 35:480-92 (August 1973).

Laslett, Peter. **The World We Have Lost.** New York: Charles Scribner's Sons, 1971.

Leichter, Hope Jensen, ed. **The Family as Educator.** New York: Teachers College Press. 1974.

_____, and Mitchell, William E. **Kinship and Casework.** New York: Russell Sage Foundation, 1967.

Leslie, Gerald R. **The Family in Social Context.** New York: Oxford University Press, 1973.

Leupnitz, Deborah A. "The Effects of Divorce on Children: A Review of the Literature With Implications for Psychology and Law." Paper written at State University of New York at Buffalo, April 1976.

Levine, Murray, and Levine, Adeline. **A Social History of Helping Services.** New York: Appleton-Century-Crofts, 1970.

Lindblom, Charles E. **The Policy-Making Process.** Englewood Cliffs, N.J.: Prentice-Hall, Inc., 1958.

Lourie, Norman V. "Presidential Address to the National Conference on Social Welfare." Paper presented at the National Conference on Social Welfare, Washington, D.C., 13-17 June 1976.

Lurie, Harold L., ed. **Encyclopedia of Social Work.** New York: National Association of Social Workers, 1965, p. 941.

Mace, David, and Mace, Vera. **We Can Have Better Marriages If We Really Want Them.** Nashville, Tenn.: Abingdon Press, 1974.

McGinnis, Thomas C., and Ayres, John U. **Open Family Living.** Garden City, N.Y.: Doubleday, 1976.

McKnight, John L. "Colloquium on the Family." Paper presented at the Annual Meeting of the Central and Midwest Regional Councils of Family Service Association of America, Chicago, 29 March 1976.

McLaughlin, Virginia Yan. "Patterns of Work and Family Organization:

Buffalo's Italians." In **The American Family in Sociocultural Perspective,** edited by Michael Gordon. New York: St. Martin's Press, 1973, pp. 136-52.

Maine, Henry Sumner. **Ancient Law.** New York: Henry Holt and Co., 1888.

Manser, Gordon, and Cass, Rosemary Higgins. **Voluntarism at the Crossroads.** New York: Family Service Association of America, 1976.

"Marriage, Family Stability, and Economic Well-Being." **ISR Newsletter,** 4:1-4 (Spring 1976).

Maxey, David. "No More Messiahs, Please." **Psychology Today,** 8:123 (October 1974).

Metropolitan Life Insurance Company. "Trends in Expected Family Size in the United States." **Metropolitan Life Statistical Bulletin,** January 1975, pp. 10-11.

Mondale, Walter F. "A Family Impact Statement—A Response from the U.S. Senate." **School Review,** November 1974, pp. 11-14.

Morris, Earl W., and Winter, Mary. "A Theory of Family Housing Adjustment." **Journal of Marriage and the Family,** 37:79-88 (February 1975).

Mott, Paul E. **Foster Care and Adoptions: Some Key Policy Issues.** Washington, D.C.: U.S. Government Printing Office, 1975.

Moynihan, Daniel P. "A Family Policy for the Nation." In **The Moynihan Report and the Politics of Controversy,** edited by Lee Rainwater and William L. Yancey. Cambridge, Mass.: The M.I.T. Press, 1967.

_____. "Policy vs. Program in the '70's." **The Public Interest,** 90-100 (Summer 1970).

_____. **The Negro Family: The Case for National Action.** Washington, D.C.: U.S. Department of Labor, Office of Policy Planning and Research. March 1965.

_____.**The Politics of a Guaranteed Income.** New York: Vintage Books, 1973.

Myrdal, Alva. **Nation and Family.** Cambridge, Mass.: The M.I.T. Press, 1968.

National Easter Seal Society for Crippled Children and Adults. "Testimony before the Senate Subcommittee on the Handicapped," 23 February 1976.

Nickel, George D. Memorandum to Executives and Presidents of Accredited and Provisional Member Agencies, Family Service Association of America, 28 June 1974.

Norton, Susan L. "Marital Migration in Essex County, Massachusetts, in the Colonial and Early Federal Periods." **Journal of Marriage and the Family,** 35:406-18 (August 1973).

Novak, Michael. "The Family Out of Favor." **Harper's Magazine,** 252: 37-46 (April 1976).

Oberheu, Howard. "The Typical Family Compared With the AFDC Family." **Social and Rehabilitation Record,** 3:6-8 (July/August 1976).

O'Connell, Brian. "The Contribution of Voluntary Agencies in Developing Social Policies." Paper presented at the Sidney Hollander Colloquium, Council of Jewish Federations and Welfare Funds, Chicago, Illinois, 25 April 1976.

_____. "Voluntary Agencies Must Ask: What Price Independence?" **Foundation News,** 17:16-20 (July/August 1976).

Ogburn, William F. "The Changing Functions of the Family." In **Selected Studies in Marriage and the Family,** edited by Robert F. Winch and Louis Wolf Goodman. New York: Holt, Rinehart and Winston, 1968.

_____, and Tibbitts, Clark. "The Family and Its Functions." In **Recent Trends in the United States,** edited by the President's Research Committee on Social Trends. New York: Whittlesey House, 1934.

Otto, Herbert A. **Marriage and Family Enrichment : New Perspectives and Programs.** Nashville, Tenn.: Abingdon Press, 1976.

Parsons, Talcott. "The Social Structure of The Family." In **The Family: Its Function and Destiny,** edited by Ruth N. Anshen. New York: Harper and Bros., 1959.

Perlis, Leo. "The Human Contract in the Work Place." **Family Service Highlights,** 6:5–6 (September-October 1976).

Pringle, Bruce M. "Family Clusters as a Means of Reducing Isolation Among Urbanites." **The Family Coordinator,** 23:175-79 (April 1974).

"Quantifying the Unquantifiable." **Mosaic**, 5 (September/October 1975).

Ramey, James W. "Intimate Networks: Will They Replace the Monogamous Family?" **The Futurist**, 9:175-81 (August 1975).

"Recent Marriage and Divorce Trends Continuing." **HUD Newsletter**, 7:1 (31 May 1976).

Rice, Robert M. "A Cautionary View of Allied Services." **Social Casework**, 58:229-35 (April 1977).

_____."Impact of Government Contracts on Voluntary Social Agencies." **Social Casework**, 56:387-95 (July 1975).

Rich, Margaret E. **A Belief in People.** New York: Family Service Association of America, 1956.

Riley, Patrick V. "The Family Service System: Unity Within Diversity." Paper presented at the Biennial Conference of Family Service Association of America, Boston, Mass., 27 October 1975.

"Robert M. Rice Heads New FSAA Policy Division." **Family Service Highlights**, 2:2 (September 1975).

Romanyshyn, John M. **Social Welfare: Charity to Justice.** New York: Random House, 1971.

Ross, Heather L., and Sawhill, Isabel V. **Time of Transition: The Growth of Families Headed by Women.** Washington, D.C.: The Urban Institute, 1975.

Ryan, William. **Blaming the Victim.** New York: Pantheon Books, 1971.

Scanzoni, John. **The Conjugal Family and Consumption Behavior.** Bryn Mawr: The McCahan Foundation, 1968.

Schnaiberg, Allan, and Goldenberg, Sheldon. "Closing the Circle: The Impact of Children on Parental Status." **Journal of Marriage and the Family**, 37:937-53 (November 1975).

Schorr, Alvin L. "Family Values and Real Life." **Social Casework**, 57:397-404 (June 1976).

Sheinbein, Marc. "Normal Crises: Stage Theory and Family Therapy." **Journal of Family Counseling**, 4:78-83 (Spring 1976).

Sherman, Edmund A.; Phillips, Michael H.; Haring, Barbara L.; and

Shyne, Ann W. **Services to Children in Their Own Homes: Its Nature and Outcome.** New York: Child Welfare League of America, 1974.

Shorter, Edward. **The Making of the Modern Family.** New York: Basic Books, 1975.

"Shriver Announces Comprehensive Program to Restore the Authority of American Families." **Shriver for President.** News release, Des Moines, Iowa, 15 January 1976.

Smith, Daniel Scott. "Parental Power and Marriage Patterns: An Analysis of Historical Trends in Hingham, Massachusetts." **Journal of Marriage and the Family,** 35:419-28 (August 1973).

Smith, David M. **The Geography of Social Well-Being in the United States.** New York: McGraw-Hill, 1973.

Spark, Geraldine M., and Brody, Elaine M. "The Aged are Family Members." **Family Process,** 9:195-208 (June 1970).

Staples, Robert. "Public Policy and the Changing Status of Black Families." **The Family Coordinator,** 22:345-51 (July 1973).

Stolte-Heiskanen, Veronica. "Family Needs and Societal Institutions: Potential Empirical Linkage Mechanisms." **Journal of Marriage and the Family,** 37:903-16 (November 1975).

Sussman, Marvin B. "Family." **Encyclopedia of Social Work,** vol. 1. New York: National Association of Social Workers, 1971.

_____. "Family, Kinship and Bureaucracy." In **The Meaning of Social Change,** edited by Angus Campbell and Philip E. Converse. New York: Russell Sage Foundation, 1972.

_____. "Family Systems in the 1970's: Analysis, Policies and Programs." **The Annals of the American Academy,** 396:40-56 (July 1971).

Swain, Karl L. "Marriages and Family Counselor Licensure: Special Reference to Nevada." **Journal of Marriage and Family Counseling,** 1:149-55 (April 1975).

"Testimony of Marian Wright Edelman on the Child and Family Services Act." **Congressional Record,** 22 February 1975, 524–28. Washington, D.C.: U.S. Government Printing Office.

The Federal Constitution of the Swiss Confederation. Article 34, Section 1. Unofficial translation.

The New York Times. "Census Finds Adults Wed Later, Divorce Sooner." 8 January 1976.

_____. "Panel Urges Moves to Shore Up Family and Protect Poor children." 15 December 1976.

The Roper Organization, Inc. **The Virginia Slims American Women's Opinion Poll,** vol. III. New York: The Roper Organization, 1974.

Toffler, Alvin. **Future Shock.** New York: Random House, 1970.

Udry, J. Richard. **The Social Context of Marriage.** Philidelphia: J.B. Lippincott Co., 1966.

United Nations Secretariat. **Trends in Social Conditions and Policies in Europe,** Working Paper I. Geneva: United Nations, 1974. (Mimeo-graphed.)

U.S. Bureau of the Census. **Statistical Abstract of the U.S.: '75.** Washington, D.C.: U.S. Government Printing Office, 1975.

U.S. Department of Commerce, Bureau of the Census. "Household Money Income in 1974 and Economic Characteristics of Households." **Current Population Reports.** Series P-60, No. 100. Washington, D.C.: U.S. Government Printing Office, 1975.

U.S. Senate, Committee on Labor and Public Welfare. **American Families: Trends and Pressures, 1973.** Washington, D.C.: U.S. Government Printing Office, 1974.

U.S. Senate, Subcommittee on Children and Youth of the Committee on Labor and Public Welfare. **Background Materials Concerning the Child and Family Services Act, 1975.** S. 626. Washington, D.C.: U.S. Government Printing Office, 1976.

Vanier Institute of the Family. **Some Policy Approaches of the Vanier Institute of the Family.** Ottawa, Ontario: The Vanier Institute of the Family, June 1974.

_____. "The New Life." Draft of a report of the Vanier Institute of the Family, 1975.

Walker, E. Jerry. " 'Til Business Us Do Part?" **Harvard Business Review,** 94-101 (January-February 1976).

Wilensky, Harold L., and Lebeaux, Charles N. **Industrial Society and Social Welfare.** New York: Russell Sage Foundation, 1958.

Winch, Robert F. **The Modern Family.** New York: Holt, Rinehart and Winston, 1971.

Wolfensberger, Wolf. "Toward Citizen Advocacy for the Handicapped, Impaired, and Disadvantaged." Paper prepared for National Institute of Child Health and Human Development, Washington, D.C., 1971.

Yankelovich, Skelly, and White, Inc. **The General Mills American Family Report, 1974-75.** Minneapolis, Minn.: General Mills, Inc., 1975.

_____. **The General Mills American Family Report, 1976-77.** Minneapolis, Minn.: General Mills, Inc., 1977.

Young Families in the Society. Paris: International Union of Family Organizations, 1969.

Zimmerman, Shirley. "The Family and Its Relevance for Social Policy." **Social Casework,** 57:547-55 (November 1976).

INDEX